BEYOND ROOTS:

IN SEARCH OF BLACKS IN THE BIBLE

BY
WILLIAM DWIGHT MCKISSIC, SR.

Foreword By
Dr. Anthony T. Evans

CONTENTS

PART I
THE BIBLICAL ROOTS OF THE NEGRO

PART II
THE BIBLICAL FAITH OF THE NEGRO

ACKNOWLEDGEMENTS

To Mrs. Edna Wilkins, a devoted public school and Sunday school teacher: Thank you for typing this book as a labor of love.

To my precious wife, Vera, and our children, Dwight Jr., J.E., Carla and Michelle: Thank you for your patience while I penned these pages.

To Rev. Bob Fowler and Rev. Raymond Bishop: Thank you for listening to these ideas as they were being formed, providing critical feedback and assisting me with research.

To my parents, Rev. and Mrs. J.E. McKissic: Thank you for leading me to place my faith in Jesus Christ so that I might be rooted and grounded in Him.

To my brother, Rev. Ray E. McKissic: You were the first major influence in my life in the realm of exegetical Bible study and expository preaching.

To the Cornerstone Baptist Church of Arlington: Thank you for providing the laboratory, love and support that allowed me to develop these ideas and complete this book.

To the Glory of God, who would have all men saved and come to the knowledge of the truth.

FOREWORD

Some years ago the entertainment world was held spellbound by the T.V. series "Roots." At the heart of the series' theme was the underlining question of Black identity. The question was not only posed by the African slave who had to establish a new sense of identity on the shores of slave America, but it was also the question of the slave owners who had to come to grips with this stranger from afar.

James Baldwin's famous novel *Nobody Knows My Name* would be an appropriate rendering of the identification perspective of the slave owners who refused to recognize the identity of this new presence.

Hundreds of years since the first arrival of slaves to these shores, the issue of identity is still very much with us. It is visibly seen in the new description the African has passed through, from colored to Negro to Black to African American. It is also visibly seen in the rejection and continued disenfranchisement of Blacks by many whites and the inability to get beyond the issue of color.

Unfortunately, the problem is as replete in the church as it is in the secular community. In fact, it is often worse. Why is this? I would like to posture that it is primarily because of the failure of Christians to approach the issue of race from a theological rather than simply an anthropological perspective. This theological failure has kept us from appealing to the source of race from whom every family under heaven receives its name (Ephesians 2:15). God has too often been left out of the debate. He has been left out either by omission where all the data has not been gathered or by commission where the data that is gathered is presented to provide justification and maintenance to existing non-Christian cultural standards (i.e., the Curse of Ham).

This work by Rev. William Dwight McKissic deals squarely with the issue of race from an exegetically based, isagogical accurate perspective. His conclusions are true to the text and context of Scripture. Because of the Christo-centric approach of Rev. McKissic, honoring the Lord takes residence over honoring His culture or, for that matter, any other culture. Rev. McKissic shows conclusively that Black people (or African Americans if you prefer) do have an identity rooted in God. To the degree that we reject or accept the root of that identity is the degree to which we can know who we are. The author refutes arguments that seek to demean God's creative genius in the creation of Black people while at the same time maintaining the creator/creature distinction lest we as African Americans think more of ourselves than we ought.

Rev. McKissic's ability for conciseness has allowed a very thick book in content to be placed in a rather compact package. Any Black person who reads this work will be able to shout to God: "I am fearfully and wonderfully made." Any non-Black who reads it will begin a biblical search for their own roots.

Dr. Anthony T. Evans

PREFACE

This book is simply the effort of one Black brother to say to another Black brother there is a biblical and historic ethnic link between the Christian faith and the Black race that predates slavery in America; therefore, we should strengthen and develop that bond and not be seduced by any other doctrine. I present this brief work praying that through it the Holy Spirit will draw persons who have heretofore rejected Christ and Christianity, perhaps because of questions and concerns related to race and the Christian faith, to commitment and faith in the Lord Jesus Christ. I make no claims to being a scholar, theologian, anthropologist, historian, linguist or scientist; yet, I have labored diligently to be biblically based, theologically true, anthropologically accurate, historically honest, etymologically enlightening and scientifically sound. I am a preacher of the gospel of the Lord Jesus Christ; therefore, I make no apologies for preaching at certain points in this manuscript (particularly in chapters 7 and 8), because I have a case of the "can't help its" -I cannot help but preach those things I have seen and heard (Acts 5:20).

I am deeply indebted to all who have blazed this trail before me. I have sought to give credit to whom credit is due in the bibliography. This book reflects the toil and tears of numerous writers and speakers whose efficiency and eloquence have inspired and informed me. Many of them are lost from memory and are quoted here without citation. Without their work, I would have been unable to provide answers to questions that have concerned many regarding race and the Bible.

It is my desire that these pages inspire others to explore the ethnic factor in Scripture, Christian history and contemporary society. This information is edifying, encouraging, inspiring and interesting to those of us who believe and are curious about the role of the Black man in biblical and historical Christianity.

The fact that people of color have played an extremely important role in biblical and classical Christianity has been a neglected factor in theological education. Collectively, three of my closest friends and I have over twenty years of college and seminary training under our belts. Before this study, none of us could answer biblically or definitively basic questions such as: Were there Black characters in the Bible? If so, who were they and what roles did they play? Were any of the biblical writers Black? If so, which one(s)? Was Ham (Noah's son) Black? If so, how did Ham get his complexion? Were Black people ever cursed in Scripture? Were any of the early church fathers Black? What role did Africa and Africans play in the New Testament and post-New Testament Christianity? What color was Jesus? Did Black people receive Jesus Christ during slavery in America or prior to slavery? What was the role and identity of the Black man in ancient history? Our colleges and seminaries graduate people every year who cannot answer these basic questions. Knowing the answers to these questions can be extremely helpful if your primary ministry responsibility is to evangelize and educate Black people. If you think the answers to these questions are unimportant or irrelevant, please read chapter 1 carefully. However, permit me to say at this point that the answers to these questions are important to all people because, biblically speaking, our origin and heritage are inextricably combined and woven together, regardless of our complexions. The Dallas City Council discussed the ethnicity of Jesus as it related to the controversial film "The Last Temptation of Christ." If politicians wrestle with the ethnicity of Jesus, certainly preachers should be knowledgeable about biblical ethnicity.

A people ignorant of their history is like a tree without roots. If you do not know your history, you do not know your destiny. If we can discover some positive things about our past in Scripture and early Christian history, it would certainly make a positive impact upon our present pilgrimage. I pray that you find this work informative and edifying. I present this work in Christ's name and for His glory.

PART I

THE BIBLICAL ROOTS
OF THE NEGRO

CHAPTER I

Introduction: In Search of Blacks in the Bible

In his book, *THE GOSPEL FOR THE GHETTO*, Dr. Manuel L. Scott provides us with an interesting, arresting and even humorous assessment of Negro religion. Dr. Scott quotes Dr. Vernon Johns, a Black pastor who preceded Dr. Martin Luther King Jr., as pastor of the historic Dexter Avenue Baptist Church in Montgomery, Alabama. Dr. Johns had this to say about Negro religion:

Negro religion is 40 percent emotionalism, 30 percent hilarity, 28 percent hysteria and 2 percent miscellaneous.

Obviously, Dr. Johns did not intend for his assessment to be taken seriously, but he raises an interesting issue. What about Negro religion? What about the Negro? Does the Bible give us any insight into the racial and religious heritage of Black people? Is the Judeo-Christian faith the historic religion of Negro people or are the Black Muslims correct when they assert that Blacks were first introduced to Christianity in America by the white man as a means of making the slaves docile?

Alex Haley did a fantastic job of tracing his family roots, but the questions that kept haunting me were related to my biblical ethnic roots.

In September 1987, I launched a series of sermons based on the book of Genesis. When I arrived at Genesis 10, I recognized that inherent in that chapter were answers to questions that had concerned me for years. I discovered that Genesis 10 was the key that could unlock the door to biblical ethnicity. For the next fifteen months, whenever I could find ample time, I studied Genesis 10 to the best of my ability, particularly verses six through twenty. This book is a brief summary of my study.

My thesis is that Negro Christianity did not begin in America with the "Christianizing" of the slaves; but rather, it is deeply rooted in the Judeo-Christian heritage from the time of Noah to today. My purpose is to inform the general reader about biblical ethnicity, identify the Negro in Scripture and Christian history in order to refute the Black Muslims' belief that "Islam is the natural religion of the Black Nation," and to inspire contemporary Negroes to convert to Christ and strengthen their relationship with Him.

To begin this summary, I deem it absolutely necessary to provide you with ten foundational, positional statements that are designed to articulate the significance of this subject matter, enhance its interpretation and protect the stated purposes of this book.

The questions that inevitably arise when the subject of biblical ethnicity is brought to the forefront are: Does it really matter? Is the question of ethnic identity in Scripture important? I offer four responses to these questions as part of the ten foundational/positional statements that should serve as guidelines for the interpretation of this book:

[1] BIBLICAL ETHNICITY IS IMPORTANT TO THOSE OF US WHO ARE CHARGED WITH THE RESPONSIBILITY OF PREACHING THE "WHOLE COUNSEL OF GOD" (ACTS 20:27; II TIMOTHY 4:2).

It is impossible to preach the word of God in its entirety without coming to grips (exegetically and expositionally) with the ethnic factor in Scripture. It is certainly impossible to preach Genesis 9 and 10 without dealing with the subject of biblical ethnicity.

{2] BIBLICAL ETHNICITY IS IMPORTANT TO THOSE OF US WHO HAVE BEEN CHARGED WITH THE RESPONSIBILITY OF EVANGELISM (II TIMOTHY 4:5) AND APOLOGETICS (DEFENDING THE FAITH, I PETER 3:15; JUDE 3).

Peter taught that Christians are to respond rationally and respectfully to all who ask questions about our faith in Christ. There are issues related to the ethnic factor in Scripture that sometimes place hurdles in evangelism, particularly when people of color are being evangelized. I personally believe that in a world that is two-thirds populated by people of color, it is unwise to ignore biblical ethnicity. One reason that the Islamic faith is sweeping the world today is because many people of color (from a global perspective) historically and ethnically identify with Islam. However, a study and recognition of the ethnic factor in Christianity could once and for all put the idea to rest that "Islam is the natural religion of the Black man."....

[3) BIBLICAL ETHNICITY IS IMPORTANT TO THOSE OF US WHO ARE CHARGE D WITH THE TASK OF CHRISTIAN EDUCATION (MATTHEW 28:16-20).

A study of the ethnic factor in Scripture has greatly increased my knowledge of biblical backgrounds, biblical and historical theology, archaeology, anthropology, linguistics and church history, and I believe it will do the same for others. Biblical ethnicity is important in the realm of sacred and secular education, particularly as it relates to the origin, identity and development of the races of mankind. Recently, a poll revealed that the majority of high school biology teachers in America believe that certain races are inherently inferior to others, and *Newsweek* reported that many Chinese "adhere to racial hierarchy in which the darker a person's skin color, the lower his status and worth." These beliefs clearly indicate that biblical teaching regarding racial origins, geographic roots, ethnic heritage, equality before God (Malachi 2: 10; Acts 10:34), and oneness in Christ (Galatians 3:28) is desperately needed.

[4] BIBLICAL ETHNICITY IS IMPORTANT IN THE REALM OF RACE RELATIONS.

There is a resurgence of racism in our land. Many address racial issues with emotions rather than information -"heat rather than light." Because the subject of biblical ethnicity has been largely ignored in Christian education, ignorance abounds. Ignorance is at the core of racism. This study is important because it will address the subject of race from the standpoint of information rather than emotion -"light rather than heat." This "light" could help to drive out the darkness of racism.

[5] THE PRIMARY SOURCE FOR CONCLUSIONS DRAWN IN THIS BOOK IS THE BIBLE.

As far as I am concerned, any legitimate study of mankind must have as its base and ultimate boundary the Bible, which I believe to be the infallible word of God. I agree with Dr. James T. Draper:

> The Bible is not a scientific textbook, but everywhere the Bible touches upon scientific fact, it is without error. It is not a history book, but all historical events recorded are true.

Included in the ethnological, genealogical and geographic table of Genesis 10 are some theological and historical truths worthy of our consideration. If Genesis 10 is not the first record of the origin and development of the races of mankind, it is certainly the only accurate and authentic record of the origin and geographic distribution of the races of mankind. It is amazing what we can learn about the origin and history of the races of mankind by studying God's textbook. All Scripture quotations, unless otherwise noted, are from the King James version of the Bible.

[6] THE PRIMARY EXTRABIBLICAL SOURCE THAT SHAPED MY THINKING WAS A BOOK ENTITLED *NOAH'S THREE SONS (HUMAN HISTORY IN THREE DIMENSIONS), BY DR. ARTHUR C. CUSTANCE.*

Dr. Custance holds a Ph.D. in Anthropology and an M.A. in Oriental Studies. His book was published by Zondervan Press in 1975. In my opinion, Dr. Custance's book should be on the required reading list of every high school and college throughout the world. For persons of all races interested in an objective general history of the races of mankind from an ethnic viewpoint, I highly recommend Dr. Custance's book.

[7] I AM IN NO WAY ATTEMPTING TO PROMOTE BLACK SUPERIORITY OR INFERIORITY, CAUCASIAN SUPERIORITY OR INFERIORITY, OR SEMITIC SUPERIORITY OR INFERIORITY.

However, I can assure you that statements will be made (if taken out of context and with disregard for the stated purposes of this book) that could easily cause one to make any of the aforementioned assumptions.

[8] I AM ATTEMPTING TO PROMOTE THE SUPREMACY OF JESUS CHRIST.

If Christ is exalted and men and women come to see Him in a new light as a result of this effort, then this book will have achieved its objective.

[9] I USED THE TERMS AFRICAN, HAMITIC, BLACK AND NEGRO INTERCHANGEABLY.

I realize that this is an oversimplification in some instances, but I have sought to clarify these terms throughout this discourse, particularly in chapter 9. The reader may choose the term which less offends his or her sensibilities. The final chapter of this book is devoted to a summary and review of name designations for dark-skinned persons from the beginning of time to the present hour. For those of us who know the Lord, I discuss our name designation in the ages to come.

[10] I AM SOMEWHAT GIVEN TO "RABBIT CHASING."

I have tried my best throughout my ministry to employ the hermeneutical principle taught to me by Dr. Robert Dickerson, Sr.: "Be silent where the Bible is silent and speak where the Bible speaks." However, in my quest to discover whether the Black man was included in Scripture, I have had to "search the Scripture" and numerous historical and technical books. While searching, I have often found some very interesting information that I have sometimes passed along to the reader. Perhaps you will regard some of this as "rabbit chasing." As it relates to the subject of "rabbit chasing," I am reminded of a colloquial, yet classic, statement made by Dr. Tom Urrey, professor of New Testament at Southwestern Baptist Theological Seminary, in class on one occasion:

It is alright to chase a rabbit as long as that rabbit has

enough meat on it.

I realize that many will consider my search for Blacks in the Bible as a "rabbit chase," but you must admit that this rabbit has a lot of meat on it, especially for the Black man and Black evangelism. Therefore, when I pause to chase a rabbit, I hope you find enough meat on it to allow you to pardon my pursuit.

This book is divided into two parts. Part I is entitled "The Biblical Roots of the Negro." In chapter 1, I have provided a thesis statement, a purpose statement and ten foundational/ positional statements. It is very important to internalize these statements before continuing to read this book.

In chapter 2, I explore biblical teaching regarding the origin of the Negro in Scripture. In chapters 3 and 4 I identify, ethnically and geographically, the presence of the Negro in Scripture. In chapter 5, I focus on the contributions of the Negro to the biblical and ancient world.

Part II is entitled "The Biblical Faith of the Negro." In chapter 6 I provide a brief summary of the historic ethnic relationship between the Judeo-Christian faith and the Black man from the Old Testament period through this present hour. In chapter 7 I list seven prominent biblical characters who can trace their lineage to Ham. In chapter 8 I respond to three major criticisms that Black Christians sometimes face when sharing their faith. Finally, in chapter 9 I summarize this book by reviewing name designations for dark-skinned persons from the beginning of recorded history through the modern period. For those of us who know the Lord, I discuss our most important name designation.

In conclusion, if this book is used by God to strengthen the historic bond between Black people and the Judeo-Christian faith, to equip the church to reach those who have rejected Christ and Christianity because of ethnic concerns and to educate those in the family regarding biblical ethnicity, then this work will have fulfilled its purpose. With that said, let us begin our search.

CHAPTER 2

Ham: Noah's Negro Son

Have you ever given thought to the origin, identity and role of the Negro in early biblical history and the ancient world? Scripture, science and secular history attest to the fact that dark-skinned people were politically, culturally and numerically dominant in the ancient world and were the fathers of civilized society as we know it today. By "ancient world," I mean the period in history from the time of Noah after the flood (4000 B.C.) to the conquest of most of the known world by the Greeks under Alexander the Great (321 B.C.). However, one of the best kept secrets in all of history is the identity, role and prominence of the Negro in the ancient world. The purpose of this chapter is to identify the Negro in Scripture and to highlight his contribution to the biblical and ancient world.

The Ethnicity of Ham

The Bible clearly teaches that all mankind derived from Noah and his sons (Acts 17:-26; Genesis 9:18-19). Noah had three sons named Ham, Shem and Japheth. The name Ham means "dark or black," Shem means "dusky or olive-colored," and Japheth means "bright or fair." Biblical scholars, and at least one prominent anthropologist, consider Ham to be the ancestral father of Negroes, Mongoloids and Indians; Shem is considered to be the ancestral father of Semites (Arabic and Jewish); and Japheth is considered to be the ancestral father of Caucasians. Are the scholars correct? Based on the etymology of the three sons' names, the nations associated with their names in Genesis 10, historical research and biblical authority, I am inclined to agree with the scholars: Noah's three sons were the progenitors of the three basic races of mankind. The Bible says, "These are the three sons of Noah: and of them was the whole earth overspread" (Genesis 9:19). Even though I recognized that the three basic complexions of the three races of mankind are implicit in the names of Noah's sons, I was puzzled as to how a monogamous Noah could produce three sons of three different complexions and, consequently, ethnic identities. This seemed biologically impossible to me.

According to Burnett Hanson, M.D., it is possible for a man to father three children with three different complexions -one "black or dark," another "dusky" or "olive-colored," and the third "bright or fair" -by the same woman. Dr. Hanson further adds, "In order for this to take place, either the man or his wife has to be dark complexioned or both of them could have been dark. Dark-skinned people can and often do produce fair complexioned offspring; however, it is genetically impossible for bright or fair complexioned persons to produce dark-skinned children." Based on this analysis, Dr. Hanson concludes that in order for Noah to have fathered three sons by the same woman, with all three sons having distinct complexions ranging from dark to bright, Noah or his wife had to be black or dark-skinned.

Arthur C. Custance, Ph.D. (Anthropology) seems to agree with Dr. Hanson in his book, *Noah's Three Sons*, published by Zondervan Press:

> Without becoming involved in the technicalities of genetics, it is possible that Ham may himself have been a mulatto. In fact, his name means "dark" and perhaps refers to the color of his skin. This condition may have been derived through his mother, Noah's wife, and if we suppose that Ham had himself married a mulatto woman, it is possible to account for the preservation of the negroid stock over the disaster of the flood.

Dr. Custance suggests that Ham's darkness was derived from his mother. If so, from where did his mother's darkness come? Is it possible that her darkness could have come from Adam? After all, Adam is the father of all mankind before the flood, and Noah is the father of all mankind after the flood. The Bible clearly teaches that God "Hath made of one blood all nations of men for to dwell on all the face of the earth..." (Acts 17:26). Biblical scholars universally interpret the "one blood" as a reference to Adam and/or Noah. If Ham's darkness came from his mother and his mother and father were both descendants of Adam, this raises an interesting question regarding the ethnicity of Adam and Noah. It is impossible to reach a final conclusion about the ethnicity of Ham without dealing seriously with the ethnicity of Adam and Noah.

The Ethnicity of Adam

For other reasons, I would probably find an attempt to ethnically classify Adam and Noah unnecessary, uninteresting and unwarranted. The Bible does not even make an issue of race until Genesis 9 and 10 and then only implicitly. However, for the purposes of this study and in support of my thesis, I find it of utmost interest, benefit and value to "chase this rabbit."

It is not my desire or purpose to prove that Adam was Black but that he was a man of color in order to support Dr. Hanson's position that it was absolutely necessary for a person of color to be involved in the parenting of the three major races of mankind. Let me share with you three interesting perspectives regarding the ethnicity of Adam:

1) Adam was made from dirt: "God formed man from the dust of the ground..." (Genesis 2:7). Those of us who believe in the infallibility of Scripture interpret this literally. Dirt can be a wide variety of colors, but it is usually brown, black, dark, dusky, "red" clay or sandy. The Hebrew word "dust" translated

is "aphar." The *Hebrew-Greek Key Study Bible* by Spiros Zodihates, Ph.D., gives this definition for "aphar": "dust (as powdered or gray); hence, clay, earth, mud: ashes dust, earth ground, mortar, powder, rubbish." The name Adam in Hebrew is Adham, which means "red" or taken out of red earth. Perhaps Adam was formed from "red" or clay earth. According to the *Hebrew-Greek Key Study Bible*, the name Adam means "reddish brown". I find the color "red" extremely interesting as it relates to Black and "colored" people. The renowned Black historian and scholar, Dr. W.E.B. Du Bois, made a noteworthy comment relating to the pigmentation of African people: "The primitive African was not an extreme type. One may judge from modern Pygmy and Bushmen that his color was reddish or yellow and his skull was somewhat round like the Mongolian." M.J. Herskovits says he saw African negroes who varied in color from brownish-black to reddish brown. The Greek Statius spoke of red negroes with copper colored skin. A popular "nickname" in the Black community for a Black person whose complexion is somewhere between "black and white" is "red." From an ethnic viewpoint, the color "red" has been associated with Blacks, Indians, Egyptians and Caucasians.

Based on this information, I concluded that Adam was possibly made from "red" earth, and if he were living today, he would probably be classified as "colored." Most of the people in Northeast Africa and the Middle East where Adam probably originated are classified as something other than the "white man." Furthermore, the name "Adam" is also translated to "man." Adam was the first human. The prefix "hu" in human means color. Adam, made from dirt, was a man of color.

2) Biblically speaking, Adam and Noah were Semites (Luke 3:36,38). A study of various pictures of Middle East persons claiming to be Semitic revealed that most Semitic people tend to be dusky or amber complexioned, ranging from dark to bright.

Charles Finch, an M.D. and antiquarian, states that "the

'classic' Semitic in antiquity was of a much darker hue than is true today and more closely to the Africoid type which formed the basic substratum of Western Asia." A. H. Sayce, a biblical ethnologist of the 1800s and secular anthropologist, racially classifies Semitic people as Caucasians. Thus, you see, Blacks, Whites and of course Semites have a racial affinity with Semitic people. Oh, I marvel at the wisdom of God for placing Adam and Noah in the Semitic family, for anybody who wanted to could build a case that Semitic people are "dark," "dusky" or "bright," and all three would be right.

3) Secular anthropologists and respected scientists whose findings were published in *Newsweek* and *National Geographic* have concluded that "Adam" and "Eve" were African (dark). Pictures of a Black Adam and Eve appear on the front cover of the January 11, 1988 issue of *Newsweek*. Although the scope of my study will not allow a detailed report of their findings, I must point out that, based on scientific data and research, a respected segment of the academic community believes that Adam and Eve were dark complexioned people. Again, based on biblical authority, I hold that Adam was Semitic, which means his complexion may have ranged anywhere from dark to dusky and possibly bright.

The Ethnicity of Noah

If all or any one of the points that I have tried to make in the aforementioned three perspectives regarding the ethnicity of Adam and Noah are true, it certainly explains how Noah and "Mrs. Noah" were "dusky" or "dark" and passed that darkness on to Ham. However, I differ with Dr. Custance in that Ham's darkness could have come just as easily from his father. Perhaps it is as H. G. Wells, a noted historian, stated, "Possibly the more ancient races of men were all dusky or black, and fairness is new."

22

Regardless of what the secular world concludes about the ethnicity of Adam or Noah, it is an inescapable conclusion for those of us who believe in the authority and reliability of Scripture: Adam and Eve and Noah and "Mrs. Noah" possessed the genetic makeup that produced the three basic races of mankind. I agree with St. Augustine:

> The whole human race, which was to become Adam's posterity through the first woman, was present in the first man ... whoever - is rational and mortal, regardless of color or shape or sound or voice, is certainly of the stock of Adam.

According to Scripture, Noah is the father of all mankind; therefore, he inevitably had to be the father of the Negro race. My belief, which is supported by Scripture, theologians, history, anthropology and science, is that this was done through Noah's son Ham, which is studied in the next chapter.

CHAPTER 3

The Sons of Ham

Noah's Negro son, Ham, is the father of the Black race. Ham was not cursed dark, he was born dark, which was a badge of honor to him and his people. The purpose of this chapter is to identify the sons of Ham geographically and to document their ethnicity.

Who were the sons of Ham? According to Genesis 10:6, Ham had four sons named Cush, Mizraim, Phut and Canaan. The Hamites referred to in the Bible were people who would be classified as Black or Negroid in the Western world today.

Cush (Ethiopia)

Cush was the progenitor of the Ethiopian people. The words "Ethiopia" (Genesis 2: 13) and "Cush" (Genesis 10:6) are used interchangeably in Scripture. The word "Cush" is a Hebrew word meaning "black." Ethiopia is a Greek word meaning "a man with a (sun) burned or black face." An inscription discovered in Ethiopia in 1914 has the word "Qevs" or "Kesh" in it. From this, some scholars conclude that the word "Kush" or "Cush" originated from Ethiopia rather than from Egypt or Israel. The Greek word for burned was "ethios" and the word for face was "ops," so "ethios" plus "ops" became Ethiopian.

Ethiopia is one of the first countries mentioned in Scripture (Genesis 2: 13) before and after the flood. According to Henry M. Morris, Ph.D., in his book, *The Genesis Record*, published by Baker Book House, Ethiopia was originally an antediluvian (before the flood) name and was remembered by the survivors of the flood and then given to people and places in the postdiluvian (after the flood) world in memory of the earlier name of which they were somehow reminded later. Diodorus Siculus said, "The Ethiopians conceive themselves to be of greater antiquity than any other nation." Herodotus, the father of history, maintained that the Ethiopians were the longest-lived people, "the tallest and the handsomest men in the world." The Black lady in Solomon's court described herself as Black and beautiful (Song of Solomon 1:5). Moses married an Ethiopian woman (Numbers 12:1). Dr. Du Bois records that Abyssinians (Ethiopians) are generally Black, which they most admire. The Bible describes Ethiopians as dark and tall Jeremiah 13:23; Isaiah 45:14). As a world power, the prophet Isaiah described the military men sent from Ethiopia to King Hezekiah to assure Israel of their assistance as people of "a nation tall and smooth," "a people feared near and far" and "a nation mighty and conquering" (Isaiah 18:1,2,7, RSV). Apparently, at some point in history, Ethiopian borders extended far beyond the modern day country of Ethiopia. According to Homer and Herodotus, the inhabitants of the following territories were Ethiopians: Sudan, Egypt, Arabia, Palestine, Western Asia and India. The only physical difference in these inhabitants was the texture of the hair. Dr. Du Bois claimed that Egypt was a colony of the Ethiopians. There are pyramids in Ethiopia that rival Egyptian pyramids. John G. Jackson reports that Ethiopia was the first established country on Earth. Cushites (Ethiopians) were the founders of Mesopotamian civilization. Ethiopian and Egyptian recorded history begins about 3500 B.C., which leads to a discussion of Ham's second son, Mizraim (Egypt).

Mizraim (Egypt)

The word "Mizraim" is translated in the *Revised Standard Version* of the Bible as "Egypt." According to Fausset's *Bible Dictionary*, published by Zondervan Press, the word "Mizraim" means "children of the sun."Fausset also points out that Egyptians were of a "Nigritian" origin. Egyptians did not call themselves "Egyptians"; this name was later given to them by the Greeks. Quotations from the following authors summarize my findings concerning the etymology of "Egypt" and the ethnicity of the early Egyptians:

John G. Jackson, a recognized authority on African history, wrote:

> The ancient inhabitants of this African land called the country Khem, or Kam, or Ham, which literally meant "the blackland"; and they call themselves Khemi or Kamites, or Hamites, meaning "the black people."

Keil-Delitzsch, universally respected, Old Testament, German scholars, recorded:

> The old Egyptian name is Kemi (Copt, Chemi, Kerne), which Plutarch says is derived from the ash-grey color of the soil covered by the slime of the Nile, but which is more correct to trace to Ham and to regard as indicative of the Hamitic descent of its first inhabitants.

Herodotus visited Egypt about 500 B.C. and reported:

> It is certain that the natives of the countries are black with heat...that they are black skinned and have woolly hair ...

Lerone Bennett, Jr., a contemporary Black historian, noted:

> In their paintings, the ancient Egyptians portrayed themselves in three colors: black, reddish-brown

and yellow.

Apparently, the ancient Egyptians had the same range of physical appearance as contemporary Blacks.

Mark Hyman, a Black journalist and historian, reveals scientific documentation as to the ethnicity of the Egyptians:

> A melanin test was taken from the skin of an Egyptian mummy ... the melanin proved the Egyptian was Black.

As far as I am concerned, the ultimate authoritative voice regarding the ethnicity of the Egyptians is found in Scripture. The Psalms refer to Egypt as the Land of Ham (Psalms 78:51; 105:23, 26-27; 106: 21-22). The name "Ham" is derived from the Egyptian name "Kam" which is the strongest word in the language for "black" or "blackness."

Many scholars readily admit that the ancient Egyptians were Black, but maintain that the Hyksos kings who ruled Egypt during a portion of this period of biblical history (1700 B.C.-1550 B.C.) were Semites from Asia. However, two eminent Black scholars oppose the position that the Hyksos were western Semites:

Dr. Charles Finch had this to say about the origin and identity of the Hyksos kings:

> It has been assumed as a matter of course that the Hyksos were Asiatic invaders from outside Egyptian territory, but the one Egyptian authority who had access to the Egyptian archives informs us only that the usurpers were of "ignoble birth" and they came "out of the eastern parts."

Nowhere does he say that they were Asiatics or came out of Asia.... Since Manetho (Egyptian historian) refers only to the "eastern parts" and not Asia, it could more logically and plausibly be assumed that he was referring to the shepherds and nomads of Egypt's eastern desert given that the name "Hyksos" is usually translated as "shepherd kings."

Dr. W.E.B. Du Bois suggests:

> The domination of Hyksos kings who may have been Negroids from Asia lasted for five hundred years. That Negroids largely dominated in the early history of western Asia is proven by the monuments.

A third Black scholar, Carter G. Woodson, lays the matter to rest once and for all:

> If the Egyptians and the majority of the tribes of Northern Africa were not Negroes, then there are no Negroes in the United States.

Finally, in the New Bible Dictionary on page 884 is a drawing of a replica of "Asiatic soldiers of the patriarchal age depicted on an Egyptian Tomb painting" that reflects distinct Negroid features, including Afro hairstyles, to aid in drawing a conclusion.

Phut (Libya)

Ham's third son was Phut. His descendants are not named in Scripture. Josephus claims that Phut was the founder of Libya and called the inhabitants Phutites. The Bible mentions Phut or Libya in the following verses: Ezekiel 27:10, 30:5, 38:5; Jeremiah 46:9; and Nahum 3:9. In Nahum 3:9, Ethiopia, Egypt, Phut (Libya) and Lubim are listed as allies of Ninevah, which certainly suggests a political and probably ethnic relationship. According to Genesis 10, all of the aforementioned nations descended from Ham. The appellation "Libya" originally meant "black."

Canaan (Palestine)

Canaan, Ham's youngest son, is perhaps associated with Ham in most Bible students' minds (more so than his older brothers) because of the curse of Canaan recorded in Genesis 9:20-26. There is no doubt about it; the Canaanites were Black. Dr. Custance recorded: "Now in the famous six-sided prism of Sennacherib, the king refers to the conquered Canaanites as 'blackness of head people.' Fausset's *Bible Dictionary* states that although it was once disputed, the fact that the Canaanites were Hamites has been proven by archaeology. The Canaanites are depicted as brown-complexioned people on Egyptian monuments.

The descendants of Ham led very advanced civilizations that predate Semitic and Jophetic civilizations by at least two thousand years, which may explain the reluctance of some scholars to identify the ancient Egyptians, Canaanites, Libyans and sometimes even the Ethiopia ns with the modern day Negro. Some scholars label these groups as white with dark skin. *Today's Dictionary of the Bible*, compiled by T.A. Bryant, states, "The race of Ham was the most energetic of all descendants of Noah in early times of the postdiluvian world." However, the only biblical heritage that some Blacks have been taught is the so-called "curse of Ham."

A careful study of Genesis 9:25-27 reveals that it was Canaan who was cursed, not Ham. Had Ham been cursed, all Blacks would have been cursed; however, in the sovereignty of God, Noah cursed Canaan for Ham's sin. Ham had four sons; only one was cursed. Like Ham, I have four children and when I spank one, the other three are not physically affected. The Bible teaches that children will suffer because of the iniquities of their parents. Canaan was cursed because of Ham's sin. The curse was a pronouncement of a particular sentence, on a particular sin, toward a particular son.

Biblically speaking, a curse lasted three or four generations (Exodus 20:5). What was the curse? Canaan was assigned servitude to Ham's brothers, Japheth and Shem. Why was Ham not cursed? According to Dr. Custance, in Hebrew thought, Noah could not have cursed Ham without cursing himself. When and how was the curse fulfilled? Most scholars believe that the curse was fulfilled when the Canaanites were conquered by Israel and became subservient to the Israelites. It is interesting to note that of Ham's four sons (Ethiopia, Egypt, Libya and Canaan), Canaan is the only one that does not exist today as a nation.

Is the curse of Ham upon the Negro today? According to Dr. J. Vernon McGhee, a distinguished conservative White Bible teacher:

> It certainly is not. To think otherwise is absolutely absurd. The Scripture does not teach it.... That teaching has been one of the sad things said about the Black man. It is not fair to the Black man and it is not fair to God-because He didn't say it. After all, the first two great civilizations were Hamitic-both the Babylonian and Egyptian civilizations were Hamitic.

I believe the curse of Canaan was fulfilled during one or all of the following experiences: (1) When certain Canaanite tribes were defeated by Abraham in Genesis 14:1-16. (2) In the days of Joshua, when Canaanites were defeated by the Israelites, who belonged to the family of Shem (Joshua, 9:23; I Kings 9:20, 21); (3) When the descendants of Canaan became the servants of Japheth when Carthage, which had been settled by the Canaanites (Phoenicians), was conquered by Rome. At any rate, the Black race has never been cursed-only the Canaanites. The Scripture also records other cursed ethnic groups and individuals.

Geographically, the Canaanites were the original inhabitants of the land of Israel (I Chronicles 4:40). This is the root cause of the modern day problem between the Palestinians and the Israelis.

CHAPTER 4

The Grandsons of Ham

Not only did Ham have four distinguished sons: Cush (Ethiopia), Mizraim (Egypt), Phut (Libya) and Canaan (Palestine), but he also had grandsons and their descendants, who were equally as prominent in the Old Testament and the ancient world. The purpose of this chapter is to further explore the lineage of Ham ethnically and geographically.

The Sons of Cush

The Bible says that the sons of Cush were Seba, Havilah, Sabtah, Raamah, Nimrod and Sabtecha, and the sons of Raamah are Sheba and Dedan (Genesis 10:7,8). These descendants of Cush settled in Southern Arabia, Northern Arabia, Ethiopia, Egypt and the Persian Gulf. In Isaiah 43:3, the name Seba is coupled with Ethiopia and in Psalm 72:16 with Sheba. Seba and Sheba are used interchangeably in Scripture and historical records. Sheba has been identified with Southern Arabia and Ethiopia. People called Sabeans (descendants of Seba) are known in Arabia and Ethiopia. Havilah (Genesis 2:13) is the first land mentioned in Scripture (excluding Eden), and Ethiopia is the second land mentioned in Scripture (Genesis 2:13). I Samuel 15:7 places Havilah near Egypt. (Sometimes we forget that Egypt is on the African continent). Raamah, Sabtah and Sabtecha all settled in Southern Arabia. Dedan settled in Northern Arabia and the Persian Gulf.

The historic and indigenous presence of the Negro in Southern Arabia and other areas of Asia is well-documented in Scripture and history. Dr. Du Bois states: "The Arabs were too nearly akin to Negroes to draw an absolute color line." Dr. Custance linked the Southern Arabians and Ethiopians together linguistically; they spoke a non-Semitic language. Emmet Russel linked Southern Arabia and Ethiopia politically. Herodotus linked these areas ethnically. II Chronicles 21:16 links Southern Arabia and Ethiopia geographically. Josephus tells us that Queen of Sheba ruled over Ethiopia and Egypt. The Keil-Delitzsch commentary tells us that Cush's son Sabtah was of the Ethiopians who peopled the Hadhramaut in Southern Arabia and looked very distinctly Negroid. Allen P. Ross notes, "The Cushites settled in Southern Arabia, and in present day Southern Egypt, Sudan, and Northern Ethiopia...Sabtah, ancient Hadhramaut, was on the western shore of the Persian Gulf." Archaeology confirms an early and perhaps indigenous presence of the Negro in the aforementioned areas.

Nimrod deserves special treatment.

Nimrod

The fact that Nimrod is a towering figure in ancient history is without question. John Phillips comments: "From the amount of space devoted to him in the Hamitic line, it is likely that he was one of the giants of the postdiluvian world." I might add that of all of the 70 names listed in the genealogical table recorded in Genesis 10, including the Japhetic and Semitic lineages, Nimrod stands alone in the biographical data given to him.

Who was Nimrod? According to Scripture, "He was the first on Earth to be a mighty man (Genesis 10:8 RSV). Phillips declares: "He became the world's first imperialist and empire builder." In Genesis 10:9, Moses recorded that Nimrod was a "mighty hunter before the Lord." Dr. J. Vernon McGhee denotes that Nimrod was not only a conqueror of animals, but also of men. The name "Nimrod" means "to subdue," "brave" and "rebel." At the time when the "whole Earth was of one language and speech" (Genesis 11:1) and traveled as a unit, Nimrod protected the Earth from wild animals and was the leader of all people on Earth. The Bible uses the word "might" three times in Genesis10: 8,9 to describe the ability of Nimrod. The Hebrew word "mighty" translated is "gibbor," which means "chief" or "chieftain." Nimrod, the grandson of Ham and the son of Cush, was the first world ruler. Unfortunately, he attempted to build the tower of Babel which was a rebellious act against God, and this is reflected in his name "rebel." Alexander Hislop, a noted European antiquarian, acknowledges that Nimrod was Black; "Now Nimrod, as the son of Cush, was Black, in other words, was a Negro." Hislop also shares that Nimrod was worshiped as a god throughout the ancient world, including Greece, until Christianity became the preeminent religion.

Shinar (Sumer)

Where did Nimrod rule? The Bible says: "And the beginning of his Kingdom was Babel and Erech" (Genesis 10:10). These are clearly Mesopotamian sites located near the Tigris and Euphrates rivers. This area was originally known as "the land of Shinar" (Genesis 10:10; 11:2). According to the *International One Volume Commentary of the Bible*, Shinar is probably the Hebrew form of Sumer. Ancient historians refer to this area as Sumer; the Bible calls this area Shinar. I find it interesting that religious and secular historians agree on at least three things about Shinar (Sumer):

1) SHINAR WAS THE STARTING POINT OF CIVILIZATION.

The Bible clearly teaches that after the flood the whole Earth was of one language and one speech, and they settled in the land of Shinar (Genesis 10:10, Genesis 11:1).

William Halo and William Kelly Simpson, professors of

ancient history at Yale University, report in their book, *The Ancient Near East*, that Shinar became the first area to produce civilization in all its essentials. "The area in question [the extreme south of Mesopotamia] may now be called Sumer, and its inhabitants Sumerians."

2) SHINAR WAS OCCUPIED PREDOMINANTLY BY BLACK PEOPLE.

Certainly, other racial groups dwelt in Shinar; however, the dominant group was Black. In the genealogical table recorded in Genesis 10, we discover that Ham had 30 descendants, Shem had 26 and Japheth had 14. Consequently, it is easy to understand why the dominant group in Shinar was Black. While all the people of the Earth were unified under Nimrod, they attempted to build a tower. (Remember, Nimrod's kingdom began at Babel (Genesis 10:10). Their stated purpose for building the tower was threefold: (1) so that the "top may reach to heaven" (religion), (2) "and let us make a name" (pride), (3) "lest we be scattered abroad" (unity). These all appear to be noble reason on the surface, but a careful study of Genesis 11:1-9 clearly reveals that these Shinar inhabitants were acting independent of God, much to his displeasure. Therefore, God confused their language and scattered them abroad. The sons of Japheth journeyed primarily to the north (Europe); the sons of Shem scattered nomadically throughout the Middle East and the sons of Ham moved primarily south into Southern Arabia, Africa and India. (I will elaborate further on the movements of these groups in chapter 5). However, the three racial groups continued to be represented in Shinar, later renamed "Babel" or "Babylon" in memory of the place where God confounded or confused their languages. (Ironically, we still refer to confused speech as babel). The dominant group of people in Shinar was the Cushites. Well-known Bible scholar Merrill F. Unger argues that southern Mesopotamia (Babel) was the original home of Hamitic Cushites. R.K. Harrison, an eminent white scholar, wrote, "About 4000 B.C., a people of superior intellectual caliber, known as Sumerians, occupied Sumer...They were a swarthy (black), non-Semitic group."

3) THE PEOPLE OF SHINAR CALLED THEMSELVES BLACK.

The Bible lists Shinar in the Hamitic family in the genealogical geographical table of Genesis 10. According to Halo and Simpson, the Sumerians referred to themselves as the "blackheaded people." Dr. Custance argues that "blackheaded people" was a reference to their skin color rather than their hair, because in this area having black hair would not have been a distinction. Runoko Rashidi, in an article entitled "More Light on Syumer, Elam and India," states: "The Sumerians did, after all, call themselves the blackheaded people, and their most powerful and pious leaders, such as Gudea of Lash, consistently chose very dark and preferably black, stone for their statutory representations." When Semitic people gained control of Sumer about 2350 B.C. under Sargon, he boasted, "The blackheaded peoples I ruled," which certainly suggests a distinction at this point between the Semitic people and the original inhabitants of Sumer. Dr. Custance maintains that in the area of the world once occupied by the Sumerians, there still remain evidence of a very dark-skinned component in the population.

Asshur

Asshur, the last descendant of Cush who was mentioned in Genesis 10, was the founder of Assyria. Clem Davies, in his book titled: *The Racial Strams of Mankind*, argues that the Assyrians were mulattoes. Asshur was the builder of the great city of Ninevah and was from the kingdom of Nimrod. Asshur also built Rehoboth, Calah and Resen (Genesis 10:11, 12), all great cities of antiquity located in Babylon. Dr. Du Bois maintains that there was a strong Negro strain among the Assyrian people.

The Sons of Mizraim (Egypt)

Ham's second son, Egypt, produced eight sons name Ludim, Anamim, Lehabim, Naphtuhim, Pathrusim, Casluhim, Phillistim and Caphtorim (Genesis 10:14). Six of Egypt's sons settled in North Africa, Caphtorim settled in Crete, and Phillistim eventually settle in southern Israel from the island of Crete. Paul's Epistle to Titus was addressed to the island of Crete (Titus 1:5). Josephus tells us that the Greeks called "Phillistim" Palestine. John Phillips notes that the word "Phillistim" is derived from an Ethiopic root. Dr. H. Beecher Hicks states that Palestinians have a genetic relationship with Black people. Appearing on the front page of the *Dallas Morning News* on January 11, 1988, are pictures of Palestinian children who are as dark as or, in two instances, darker than my four children.

Phut (Libya)

The Bible does not record any descendants for Phut. However, the name Phut, Put or Punt is prominent in African history.

Sidon (Phoenicians)

Canaan, Ham's most prolific son, had 11 descendants (Genesis 10:15-18). The Bible says Sidon was his firstborn. Sidon was located in modern Lebanon. Sidon and Tyre were the home bases for the people called Phoenicians. Josephus and Augustine, who were both eyewitnesses of the biblical and classical world, maintained that Ham's people occupied Sidon and the Phoenicians considered themselves Canaanites. The Phoenicians founded the great city of antiquity called Carthage. Bible commentator John Phillips acknowledges that "Even Carthage, the ancient rival of Rome, was not Japhetic but Hamitic...the Phoenicians were a Canaanite people."

Heth (Hittites)

Canaan's second son was Heth, the father of the Hittites. Heth's children were landowners who sold land to Abraham to bury Sarah (Genesis 23:3-20). The Hittites occupied the land of Canaan at Hebron and ruled a great empire centered in Asia Minor for over eight hundred years, apparently migrating there from Canaan. They were defeated and absorbed by an Indo-European group in Asia Minor. The Hittites were also skilled workers in timber (I Kings 5:6; 5:18). Many scholars credit the Hittites with being the early inhabitants of China. A.H. Sayce, a biblical ethnologist, describes the Hittites as having had yellow skin, and the Hittite chiefs had brown skin, black hair and dark brown eyes. The Hittites spoke a Bantu (African) language.

Jebusites

The Jebusites lived in and around Jerusalem. According to Joshua 15:63, the Jebusites were natives of Jerusalem. Although Israel conquered them, they could not expel them. Jebus was the name by which Jerusalem was known before the conquest of David.

Amorites, Girgasites, Hivites, Arkites and Sinites

The Amorites occupied the hill country of Judea at the time of the Hebrew conquest of Canaan (Joshua 10:15). The Amorites, whose name was sometimes used as a representative of all Canaanites (Genesis 15:16), were one of the most prominent tribes. The Girgasites dwelled in Canaan, but after the conquest of the Hebrews, tradition says they fled to Africa. They certainly could have ethnically identified with the Africans. The Hivites, according to *Pictorial Bible Dictionary*, were a peaceable commercial people. The Arkites were form Arka, 30 miles north of Sidon. The Sinites occupied Sin, a north Phoenician coastal town.

Biblical scholars and anthropologists have used the name "Sin," as defined in Oriental culture, to link Hamites with Mongoloid people, such as American Indians. Dr. Custance tells us that the New World was peopled by a Mongoloid racial stock, with evidence of a small Negroid component. Historians H.G. Wells and James E. Brunson document a Negro presence in early China. Even Buddha, according to Alexander Hislop, is generally represented as a Negro in China.

Arvadites, Zemarites and Hamathites

The Arvadites were located six miles south of Arvad. Sin, Arvad, Simura (Zemarites) were all town of Phoenicia. The Hamathites were located in Hamath (modern Hama) in the Orontes Valley of Syria. Perhaps the word "Hamath" is a derivative of Ham. Josephus reported in his day that "the Children of Ham possessed the land from Syria and Amanus and the mountains of Libanus, seizing upon all that was on its seacoast and as far as the ocean, and keeping it as their own." Strabo, the great geographer, reported in his day that the Syrians were Black.

Thus, we conclude our quest to identify the descendants of Ham in Genesis 10:6-20. Some may question the Hamitic roots of the people and countries listed in the lineage of Ham due to the modern day fair complexion of most of the people living in these counties. However, their modern day fair complexion can be easily explained by the fact that *all* Hamites have never been dark and the Greeks, Romans, French, Arabs and Aryans have occupied these areas for year. Furthermore, the fact that sickle-cell anemia, thalassemia and G-6-PD Deficiency (diseases uncommon to non-Mediterranean people, but common to ethnic groups from Italy, Greece, the Mediterranean Islands, India, Southeast Asia, Americans of Italian and Greek ancestry, Mid and Near Eastern areas, and of course people of African descent) could possibly suggest, from a scientific viewpoint, a genetic relationship between people of Hamitic descent listed in Genesis 10:6-20 and the aforementioned countries. I do recognize that some would attribute these common diseases to region rather than race and perhaps migration; however, the relationship between genetics, geography, disease and ethnicity is indisputable.

Theologically speaking, I concur with Allen P. Ross, professor of Semitics and the Old Testament at Dallas Theological Seminary:

This Table of Nations [Genesis 10] traces affiliation of tribes to show relationships, on the basis of some original physical connections.

God's word is true (Romans 3:4), and 4,000 years of history and research as they relate to Genesis 10, time after time affirms the accuracy and authenticity of His word.

CHAPTER 5

The Glory of Ham

Thus far, I have primarily focused on the origin and identity of the Negro in Scripture. In this chapter, I want to briefly focus on the cultural prominence of Hamites in the Old Testament world. I use the word "glory" cautiously, because glory belongs only to God. However, just as other races and nations have had and are having their "glory" years, I think it is high time we call attention to the glory years of the Negro.

The glory years of the Black man were from the beginning of civilization after the flood (4000 B.C.) during the political reign of the Semites in Mesopotamia (2350 B.C.) and Canaan (1200 B.C.). The race of Ham politically and culturally dominated the known world the first two thousand years of world history.

Geopolitical

There is a key phrase included in the Hamitic genealogical table that I believe explains the presence of dark and dusky skinned people throughout the globe at a very early date in history. IN most instances, the presence of dark skinned people throughout the world far predates the Japhetic or Semitic people. The darker races of India preceded the lighter Aryan races. The Etruscans who originated in Africa occupied Italy before the Romans. A short, swarthy (black) race initially populated France and Germany. The Aborigine of Australia, the Maoris of New Zealand, the Ainus of Japan, the Black Caribs of St. Vincent, the Olmecs of Mexico, the Jamessis of Florida, and the Garifuna of South America (the list goes on) all represent dark or dusky complexioned people who spanned the globe prior to recorded history. Columbus never set foot on what is now called the United States of America. He landed in the Bahamas (San Salvador), and there he found dark and dusky skinned people. As far as I am concerned, the significant issue of history is not Columbus' "discovery," but rather, who were the people he discovered? How did they get there? I believe the answers to these questions are found in Genesis 10:18 in ten words: "and afterward were the families of the Canaanites spread abroad."

An early and usually indigenous presence of dark and dusky complexioned people throughout the world was so easily documentable that it forced the noted historian H.G. Wells to write: "Possibly the more ancient races of men were all dusky or black, and fairness is new." The sons of Japheth were remote in the Old Testament and very little is said about them there. Recorded history for the Japhetic races does not begin until about 1000 B.C.

Rome was founded in 750 B.C. City-states in Greece did not begin until 800 B.C. The sons of Shem did not emerge as a racial or cultural group until the time of Abraham (1800-1600 B.C.). However, the sons of Ham ruled Shinar (Sumer) as early as 4000 B.C. Hamites ruled Ethiopia from 3500 B.C. to this present day. Hamites ruled Egypt from 3500 B.C. to the Persian conquest of Egypt in 525 B.C. Hamites ruled Canaan from 4000 B.C. to 1200 B.C. and Mesopotamia from 4000 B.C. to 2350 B.C. The ancient Egyptian and Sumerian peoples enslaved Japhetic, Semitic and even other Hamitic people. Seemingly the dominant group always rules the minority people. Hamites ruled India from 3000 B.C. until conquest of the Persians in 500 B.C. IN every instance, these people led extremely advanced civilization and cultures. Dr. T.B. Matson, a former professor of Christian Ethics at Southwestern Baptist theological Seminary, had this to say about the early descendants of Ham:

Those who emphasize the curse of Ham need to remember that some of the descendants of Ham, even some of the children of Canaan, were quite prosperous. They built great cities, such as Ninevah and Babylon. They were rearing palaces, digging canals, organizing governments and founding empires at a time when descendants of Japheth were wandering over Europe with no better weapons than implements of flint and bone.

Dr. Custance argued that the curse of the Canaanites was that they would spread out over the Earth and prepare the way for Shem and Jahpeth. HE further argued that they would not profit form their technological and inventive genius. Nevertheless, to the degree that this thesis may be true, it would only be applicable to the descendants of Canaan. However, it is biblically and historically irrefutable that the descendants of Ham spread abroad and ruled most of the known world during the first two thousand years of world history, paving the way for modern society.

Technology

Necessity is the mother of invention. Because the race of Ham was the most energetic of all the descendants of Noah in the early times of the postdiluvian world, the technological and creative genius demonstrated by these people even baffle modern minds. Permit me to list some of the great technological contributions of Hamites to the Old Testament world and ancient history:

Ethiopian and Egyptian Pyramids	Taming the horse
The invention of paper	Running water
Ceramics industry	Glass

Mathematics	Pulley
Engineering	Gears
Beginnings of architecture	Plans and maps
Sailing boats	Advanced embalming
Domestication of Animals	Clocks and Calendars
	(365 days)
Iron making	Food preservation
Pipe organ	

This is a partial listing of significant contributions by the ancient Hamites. Without these contributions, life would not be as it is today. All humanity owes a debt of gratitude to the ancient Hamites.

Culture

Hamitic people were not only technologically advanced, but also culturally advanced above the Semites and Japhetities in the Old Testament world. We learn from Scripture that the ancient Egyptians practiced medicine (Genesis 50:2). The Egyptians compiled the first catalogue of medicines "materia medica." Imhotep was a distinguished physician in Egyptian history. Who said Hippocrates was the founder of medicine? The Europeans developed their medical skills from the Egyptians.

Hamitic people were among the first people to have any clear conception of art other than for utilitarian purposes. Hamitic people developed the concept of city-states and were advanced in the realm of agriculture. Even in religion, they developed the concept of qualified monotheism 600 years before the Hebrews. The Hamitic Sumerians practiced law and banking 3500 years before Christ. This can be documented in a history textbook entitled World Civilizations, by Edward McNall Burns, published by W.W. Norton & Company, 1980, page 33.

A study of Old Testament and ancient history from an ethnic

and cultural perspective clearly reveals that God is no respector of persons (Acts 10:34): "And hath made of one blood all nations of men for to dwell on all the face of the Earth, and hath determined the times before appointed, and the bounds of their habitation" (Acts 17:26). Let me close this part with a quote form a contemporary white Bible teacher, Dr. J. Vernon McGhee, regarding Genesis 10 and the races of mankind:

> In chapter 10, seventy nations are listed. Fourteen of them are from Japheth. Thirty of them come from Ham. Don't forget that. It will give you a different conception of the Black man at his beginning. And twenty-six nations come from Shem...
> Why has the white man in our day been so prominent? Well, I'll tell you why. Because at the beginning it was the Black man, the colored races, that were prominent.
> Apparently, we are currently in the period in which the white man has come to the front. It seems to me that all three are demonstrating that regardless of whether they are a son of Ham or a son of Shem or a son of Japheth, they are incapable of ruling this world.

Observation: History can be divided into three dimensions. Generally speaking, each race has been given 2000 years to reign: the Reign of Ham – 4000 B.C. to 2000 B.C.; the Reign of Shem – 2000 B.C. to 300 B.C.; the Reign of Japheth – 300 B.C. to the present. What will happen when Japheth's reign is over? Could it be that we then enter into a period that I call the Reign of Jesus? John the Apostle envisioned the time when all the redeemed "of every kindred, and tongue, and people, and nation" would stand before the throne and worship Jesus (Revelation 5:9). "He which testifieth these things saith, surely I come quickly. Amen. Even so, Come, Lord Jesus" (Revelation 22:20).

PART II

*THE BIBLICAL FAITH
OF THE NEGRO*

CHAPTER 6

Christianity and the Ethiopian

In the ancient and classical world, Black people were known as Ethiopians prior to being known as Negroes. The term "Ethiopian" not only referred to the inhabitants of that ancient land, but also to dark complexioned people around the globe. Homer and Herodotus stated that the inhabitants of Sudan, Egypt, Arabia, Palestine, Western Asia and India were Ethiopians. In this chapter, I will use the term "Ethiopian" to refer to the land and people of Ethiopia and in the generic sense, as a reference to dark-skinned people everywhere. The context will determine the usage. The purpose of this section is to document the ethnic link between Ethiopian people and the Judeo-Christian faith from the days of the Old Testament to our present time. The Greeks use the term "Ethiopian" to refer to Africans who were regarded as the "burnt-faced" people.

The Biblical Roots

The following chain of events and facts trace the biblical roots of the Jewish faith as it reached the Ethiopians very early. The Ethiopian Falasha Jews who live in Ethiopia and Israel claim to be lineal descendants of Abraham. The modern day nation of Israel has granted them citizenship based on their Jewish roots. Most Ethiopians trace their Jewish roots to the Queen of Sheba and King Solomon and their alleged son Menelik. Joseph married an Ethiopian woman (Genesis 41:50-52), and their two sons (Manasseh and Ephraim) became leaders of Jewish tribes. Jethro, an Ethiopian (see chapter 7), converted to Judaism because of the testimony of Moses (Exodus 18: 1-12). Moses married an Ethiopian woman (Numbers 12:1). According to *The Bible Knowledge Commentary*, the Israelites were not forbidden to marry Cushites/Ethiopians (Exodus 34:11, 16). Jehudi (Jehudi means Jew), a secretary in the King's court during the time of Jeremiah, was a descendant of Cushi/Ethiopia (Jeremiah 36:14, 21, 23). Jehudi's grandfather's name (Cushi) literally means "black." According to David Adamo, Ph.D. (Old Testament, Baylor University), "Cushi" refers to a person of Afrian descent. Zephaniah the prophet was also a descendant of Cushi (Zephaniah 1:1). There are several Old Testament passages that underscore a unique relationship between Jehovah and the Ethiopian people:

> Are ye not as children of the Ethiopian, unto me, O children of Israel? Saith the Lord... (Amos 9:7).

> Princes shall come out of Egypt; Ethiopia shall soon stretch out her hand to God (Psalms 68:31).

> From beyond the rivers of Ethiopia my suppliants, even the daughters of my dispersed, shall bring mine offering (Zephaniah 3:10).

> And it shall come to pass in that day, that the Lord shall set his hand again the second time to recover the remnant of his people, which shall be left, from Egypt and from Pathros, and from Cush, and from Elam; and from Shinar and from Hamath, and from the island of the sea (Isaiah 11:11).

In the New Testament, there is ample biblical and historical information to affirm that the Wise Men (Matthew 2:1-12), who are often depicted as Ethiopians, are indeed Ethiopians

48

(see chapter 7). Alonzo Holly, a Black medical doctor, wrote an excellent book entitled *God and the Negro*, in which he lists Simon the Canaanite as a Negro apostle (Matthew 10:4). After all, the Canaanites were descendants of Ham. The roots of the Syrophoenician woman whose parents' faith led to her daughter's deliverance can be traced to Ham (Mark 7:24-30). Simon of Cyrene helped Jesus bear his cross (Matthew 15:21). Cyrene was a North African country. The Cyrenians shared the gospel with the Grecians, sons of Japheth Acts 11:20). The Ethiopian Eunuch was reading from a Jewish Bible in a Roman province when the Spirit of the Lord directed a Greek man to preach Jesus unto him (Acts 8:26-39). Appolos (Acts 18:24), a native of the land of Ham, was an eloquent preacher and leader in the church at Ephesus and at Corinth. Hamitic countries were represented at Penetecost (Acts 2:10,11). Simeon (Niger) and Lucius of Cyreen were leaders in the church of Antioch of Syria (Acts 11:26). Strabo reported that the Syrians were Black. It was in Antioch of Syria that Lucius and Simeon ordained and commissioned the Apostle Paul to the gospel ministry (Acts 13:2, 3). Paul's task was to take the gospel to Europe.

The Apostle Paul, in a case of mistaken identity, was classified as an Egyptian (Acts 21:38). Paul's roots can be traced to the tribe of Benjamin (Phillipians 3:5). Dr. F.S. Rhodes traces the ancestry of Benjamin to Kish (Esther 2:5) and states, "As being a descendant of a Benjaminite implied that he was of the posterity of Black people." Dr. Rhode's reference was to Mordecai, who was also a descendant of Kish the Benjaminite. Henry Morris, in his commentary on Genesis, equates Kish with Cush. The word "Kish" comes on the scene in world history as an ancient city of Mesopotamia occupied by Cushites. This evidence is far from conclusive, but no one world argue that Paul was Semitic (dusky), as opposed to Japhetic, which probably explains his being mistaken for an Egyptian.

The Classical Roots

It is an indisputable fact that Christianity experienced an early and fruitful establishment in North Africa, Egypt and Ethiopia. Dr. W.A. Criswell suggests that the roots of the Coptic Church in Ethiopia can be traced to the conversion of the Ethiopian Eunuch (Acts 8:26-39). Ethiopia is the oldest Christian country on the face of the Earth. Even when their African neighbors often converted to Islam and religion of the Middle East, Ethiopia remained faithful to the God of Abraham, Isaac and Jacob and his Son the Lord Jesus Christ. The North African and Ethiopian churches were the leading churches in the second century.

At least nine of the eighteen or twenty most prominent leaders in post New Testament Christianity were African. They included Clement, Origen, Tertullian, Cyprian, Dionysius, Athanassius, Didymus, Augustine and Cyril. Augustine is recognized as the father of theology. He authored many outstanding books, including *The City of God* and *Confessions of St. Augustine*. He was also the Bishop of Hippo, a North African region. Origen was born in Alexandria, Egypt. He understood the Scripture to be literally relevant to every situation; therefore, he did not possess two coats or wear shoes because of Jesus' words in Matthew 10:7-10. He was a prolific writer and a powerful preacher and was ordained an elder in Palestine around 230 A.D. Tertullian, born in Carthage, Africa, named and explained the Trinity. Tertullian was one of the greatest of the early church apologists. The people of Carthage, North Africa and Egypt were unquestionably dark complexioned before the conquest of the Arabs in the seventh century A.D. Anthropology supports this conclusion.

The Modern Historical Roots

In American history, the great tradition of outstanding Christian leaders, preachers and thinkers was carried on by people like Richard Allen, John Jasper, Absolom Jones and Lott Carey. Richard Allen was the founder of the African Methodist Church. John Jasper was one of the best-known preachers of his time. Lott Carey returned to Africa as a missionary; a missionary convention named in his honor exists today. Modern day children of the Ethiopians in America are continuing to fulfill the Davidic prophecy that Ethiopia would stretch out her hand to God (Psalms 68:31). Some examples are:

The National Baptist Convention, under the leadership of Dr. T.J. Jemison, has constructed a mega-modern $12 million headquarters in Nashville, Tennessee. Dr. E.V. Hill preaches to millions weekly with his national T.V. ministry on T.B.N.

Dr. Anthony Evans, through his national Urban Alternative Radio Ministry, daily impacts the lives of thousands of Christians and non-Christians in urban areas. Dr. J. Alfred Smith has strengthened pastors and churches throughout America with his prolific writing ministry. Dr. Sid Smith, who serves as a consultant with the Southern Baptist Sunday School Board, has been very effective in helping Black churches across the nation to shift from teacher oriented Sunday schools to growth-oriented Sunday schools.

Dr. C.A.W. Clark and Rev. Jerry Black, through their National Revival Ministries, travel this nation leading congregations in renewal and revival. Evangelists Randal Miller and Manuel Scott Jr. serve with distinction as successful full-time vocational evangelists. Rev. E.K. Bailey and Dr. Joe Ratliff have pioneered and popularized the staff concept in Black churches and have fully developed church program ministries.

Pastors A.L. Patterson, Frederick Haynes and Maurice Watson provide national models in the realm of expository preaching. Larnell Harris and Dr. Vernard Johnson have impacted our nation with cross-cultural music ministries.

Pastor N.L. Robinson of the Mt. Olive Baptist Church in Arlington, Texas; Pastor H. Beecher Hicks of the Metropolitan Baptist Church in Washington, D.C.; and Pastor Charles Jackson of the Pleasant Grove Baptist Church in Houston, Texas, have led their congregations to construct church facilities that can be described as architecturally and aesthetically "awesome," monumental and mammoth in size and significance, and structurally designed to minister to the whole man.

Pastor Fred Price and the Crenshaw Christian Center have erected a 10,000-seat sanctuary in Los Angeles, California.

The roots of Black Christianity can be traced from Solomon to Simon of Cyrene (see chapter 7), from Augustine to Allen (Richard), and from Jasper (John) to Jemison (T.J.). THE ETHIOPIANS ARE INDEED STRETCHING OUT THEIR HANDS TO GOD (Psalms 68:31).

CHAPTER 7

Guess Who's Coming to Dinner

Those of us over thirty years of age will recall a motion picture from yesteryear titled, "Guess Who's Coming to Dinner." The details of the movie have long since escaped my memory but I do recall that Sidney Poitier was the surprise dinner guest of a wealthy white family and also engaged to the only daughter in the family. Indeed, those parents were in for quite a surprise. If you and I were able to host a dinner and invite some of our favorite Bible characters, we may be equally surprised by the ethnic identity of some of the characters that accept our invitation. Would you be surprised if a dark-skinned man showed up?

Grolier Encyclopedia states that Negroes' skin color is typically dark brown but is often black and is yellowish brown in some groups. *World Book Encyclopedia* states: "In the United States, any person known to have a Negro ancestor is usually classified as a Negro, even though his skin may be white." Persons of any known degree of Negro ancestry in the United States can classify anyone in Scripture whose lineage can be traced to Ham and his descendants as a Negro. In this chapter, I want to identify seven prominent Bible characters whose roots can be traced to Ham. However, I do not mean to suggest in every case that these persons were all Black. Four of these characters would be predominantly Semitic as opposed to Hamitic, but a study of their roots documents a Hamitic presence in tier family trees. It has been suggested that the blood of a Negro is like the blood of Jesus – "One drop makes you whole." The only reason that I raise this issue is to refute the position sometimes found in the Black community that there is no historic ethnic link between Christianity and the Black community. This position is often a tremendous obstacle to those of us who seek to win our Black brothers and sisters to Jesus Christ. This list is obviously selective. Who are seven of my favorite Bible characters that would show up? Jethro, Joshua, David, Solomon, the Wise Men, the Ethiopian Eunuch and yes, Jesus Christ. Their ethnicities and contributions are as follows:

Jethro

Jethro was the father-in-law of Moses (Exodus 18:1). His daughter's name was Zipporah (Exodus 18:2); she is specifically identified in Scripture as an Ethiopian (Numbers 12:1). Numbers 12 records a controversy regarding Moses' marriage to this woman of Hamitic descent. Scholars argue whether the controversy had to do with her race, religion or Moses' authority.

Jethro and Zipporah were apparently proselytes to the Jewish faith (Exodus 18:7-12). *The Bible Knowledge Commentary* points out that Jews were not forbidden to marry Ethiopians (Exodus 34:11, 16). Moses and his Ethiopian wife had two sons: Gershom and Eliezer (Exodus 18:3,4).

There are three reasons why I believe Jethro was Black:

1. He was non-Semitic, leaving only two choices: Japhetic or Hamitic. Many scholars recognize that Japhetic people were remote in the Old Testament period.
2. Jethro was a Midianite. According to the *New Bible Dictionary*, page 257, Cushan [Ethiopia] was an archaic term for the Midianites (Habakkuk 3:7). John G. Jackson tells us that Midian was an Ethiopic tribe. Geographically, Midian, located in Southern

Arabia, was occupied by Cushites. According to William Leo Hansberry, professor of classical history at Howard University, derivatives of Cush such as Cushanreshathaim, Cushi, Cushite and Cushites in the Talmud and Old Testament are ethnological expressions that are traditionally considered to have been generally used over a large part of Western and Southwestern Asia in referring to Ethiopia and Ethiopian peoples. Jethro's daughter was a Cushite\Ethiopian (Numbers 12:1). Origen, the classical Christian scholar of African descent, describes Zipporah as Black and beautiful. 3. Jethro was also considered a Kenite (Judges 1:16). The Kenites were a Canaanite tribe (Genesis 15:19), descendants of Ham. Jethro worshiped the God of Israel (Exodus 18:10-12) and taught Moses how to govern God's chosen people (Exodus 18:13-27).

Joshua

Joshua is a prominent figure in Hebrew history. Joshua was the successor to Moses as leader of the Hebrew people. Under Joshua's leadership, Israel conquered Canaan/Palestine (Joshua 9), and the land was later renamed Israel. As death approached, Joshua summoned Israel's leaders together and urged them to faithfulness in conquest (Joshua 23). It was Joshua who uttered these words that hang on the outside door entrance to my house: "As for me and my house, we will serve the Lord" (Joshua 24:15). What was Joshua's link to Hamitic people? Joshua was from the tribe of Ephraim (Numbers 13:8; I Chronicles 7:22-27), who was the younger of two sons of Joseph and his Egyptian wife Asenath (Genesis 41:50-52). Ephraim was the progenitor of the tribe called by his name Joshua was descendant of Ephraim who was the son of an African woman.

It is interesting to note that Joshua's spy partner, Caleb, also had Hamitic roots. Caleb was of the tribe of Judah (Joshua 14:6, 14) and also the son of Jephunneh the Kenizzite. Judah, the progenitor of the tribe, fathered twin sons named Phaarez and Zarah (Genesis 38) by a Hamitic woman named Tamar. Japhunneh, Caleb's father, was a Kenizzite. The Kenizzites were a Canaanite tribe (Genesis 15:19). Joshua and Caleb were the two spies who went to check out Canaan and brought back the minority report (Numbers 13-14). Joshua represented Ephraim and Caleb represented Judah.

David and Solomon

David was Israel's greatest king, described in I Samuel 16 through I Kings 2:11 (I Chronicles 11-29), plus many of the Psalms. He ranks with Moses as one of the most commanding figures in the Old Testament. David's great-grandmother was Rahab, a Canaanite. Rahab is listed in the Hall of Faith (Hebrew 11) and compared to the godly patriarch Abraham in James 2:23-25. David's grandmother's name was Ruth. Ruth was a Moabite. According to the *Pictorial Bible Dictionary*, page 768, the Moabites were Canaanites. David was a light-complexioned man, particularly compared to the dark-complexioned Philistines, who were direct descendants of Ham (I Samuel 17:42; Genesis 10:14).

Solomon was the son of David by a Hamitic woman named Bathsheba. Bathsheba means daughter of Sheba, which perhaps reflects her tribal roots. In Genesis 10:7, Sheba is listed in Ham's family. Bathsheba was married to Uriah the Hittite. You may recall that the Hittites traced their roots to Ham's grandson Heth (Genesis 10:15). Solomon's complexion and hair features are described in Song of Solomon 5:10-11. This description is apparently given by the woman who described herself as "Black but beautiful" (Song of Solomon 1:5). (David Adamo, Ph.D. in Old Testament from Baylor University, states that this phrase could just as easily have been translated "Black and beautiful" and still remained true to the Hebrew text). This dark-complexioned lady described Solomon's features as follows:

My beloved is white and ruddy, the chiefest among ten thousand. His head is as the most fine gold, his locks are bushy, and black as raven (Song of Solomon 5:10, 11).

The Living Bible reads:

My beloved one is tanned and handsome, better than ten thousand others! His head is purest gold and he has wavy raven hair (Song of Solomon 5:10, 11).

The Hebrew word for "white" in the King James version is "tsach" (5:10). The definition given is "dazzling" or "sunny" or "bright." The Hebrew word translated "ruddy" in the King James version is "Adom" from the root word "Adam," which means taken out of red earth." I have already discussed the word "red" as it relates to Black people in chapter 2. I believe from these two verses we can deduce two facts regarding Solomon's physical features: (1) his head was as gold – meaning tan, dazzling, sunny, or bright and (2) his hair was black, bushy and wavy.

More importantly, Solomon was the third and last king of united Israel. He built the kingdom to its greatest geographical extension and material property. When given the choice by God to select whatever gift he wanted, he chose wisdom over wealth, longevity or the defeat of his enemies (I Kings 3:3-14). "Oh, that God would give men and women today the mind to seek his wisdom above all else. For if we receive wisdom from God, we will have the knowledge that we need to experience the abundant life" (John 10:10).

The Wise Men

The story of the Wise Men is recorded in Matthew 2:1-12. The Bible does not tell us that there were three Wise Men. It simply says, "There came wise men from the east to Jerusalem, saying, where is he that is born King of the Jews? For we have seen his star in the east, and are come to worship him" (Matthew 2:1, 2). Tradition says that there were three Wise Men perhaps because the Wise Men brought three gifts; "they presented unto him gifts; gold, and frankincense and myrrh."

Among the reason why these Wise Men, or at least one of them, have historically been depicted as a Black man, or men, are as follows:

(1) The gifts presented (gold, frankincense and myrrh) were plentiful in Southern Arabia and East Africa. Because the gifts were believed to have come from this area, the Wise Men are believed to have come from this rea. According to Dr. Custance, it was almost a universal opinion by early church fathers that the Wise Men came from Southern Arabia or possibly adjacent portions of Africa, namely Ethiopia and Somaliland. Dr. Custance further argues that Southern Arabia was largely Hamitic in origin, particularly Hadramaut and Yemen. Neither Southern Arabia nor East Africa is east of Jerusalem. The Bible says that these Wise Men came from the east and saw the star in the east (Matthew 2:1). Dr. Custance reconciles this problem by pointing out that Southern Arabia and Egypt are sometimes referred to in ancient literature as the region of the east, and the fact that they "saw his star in the east" indicates that at least for part of the journey they came from the west. According to Dr. Custance, church windows in Europe portray the Wise Men as Negroes. This tradition has

carried over to the United States with Christmas decorations depicting the Wise Men, or at least one, as a Negro.

(2) The main reason that I place some merit in the idea is because Isaiah prophesied that kings would worship him (Isaiah 18:7, particularly *The Living Bible*), Tarshish, Sheba and Seba (Psalms 72:10, 15). It is interesting to note that TArshish (Spain or one of the Mediterranean Islands) was peopled by the sons of Japheth (Genesis 10:4). Sheba and Seba (Southern Arabia and Ethiopia) were peopled by the sons of Ham and Shem (Genesis 10:7; 10:28). David envisioned the time in Psalms 72:15 when representatives of these three major races of mankind would bring gifts and worship Jesus. Perhaps this prophecy was fulfilled on the first Christmas morning.

The Ethiopian Eunuch

The Ethiopian Eunuch's nationality is obviously African. Ethnically, he is believed to be African. Dr. W.A. Criswell points out that he must have been a gifted man, for he had charge of all the treasury of the nation (Acts 8:26-39). In England, he would have been called the Chancellor of the Exchequer. In the United States, we would call him Secretary of the Treasury. He was a man of great importance and great influence.

He did not need Jesus for identification; he was identified with the head of his state as a member of her cabinet. He did not need Jesus for status. He did not need Jesus because he lacked religious faith. The Bible tells us that he left Ethiopia on his way to Jerusalem to worship (Acts 8:27). No one "brainwashed" him into accepting Christ. Surely a man of his stature could think for himself. Why did he need Jesus?

He needed Jesus to experience unconditional love. He needed

Jesus in order to be acquainted with ultimate truth and reality. He needed Jesus in order to have an eternal home. He needed Jesus for salvation. He needed Jesus for his sins to be forgiven. He needed Jesus for his conscience to be cleared. That's why I need Him.

This man is to be commended because he recognized that you can have gold without God, culture without Christ, education without salvation, a job without joy and power without peace. This man recognized that Christianity was more than a religion. A religion is simply a system of theological beliefs and practices. Almost anything can fall under the umbrella of religion and often does. Atheism is a religion. This man recognized that Christ did not come to bring us a religion but rather the truth and the whole truth about God. This man recognized that Christianity offered him an opportunity to enjoy a personal and intimate relationship with the God who created the universe, through his son Jesus Christ. This man accepted Christ, was baptized and went on his way rejoicing. He set Ethiopia aflame with the new faith he had found and Ethiopia received the gospel long before the gospel reached Europe.

OH, WHAT A WONDERFUL SAVIOUR WE'VE FOUND!

Jesus Christ

I want to make it clear that my commitment to Jesus Christ is based on content (truth), convictions based on my study of His Truth, and conversion wrought by his Holy Spirit. I would worship and serve the Lord no matter what color He is. However, to some the acceptance of a European white Jesus is totally unacceptable. Tom Skinner made an interesting statement on this subject:

Black America is not about to follow a White Christ.

The image of a Christ patterned after Sallman's portrait is more than suspect. It has become a contemptuous symbol to the Black man of all the fakery and chicanery endorsed by so many White Christians. If Christ takes on the image of an Anglo-Saxon Protestant Suburbanite, He's obviously not for Black men. It is inconceivable that this kind of Christ would die for Black people.

Skinner has summarized what I believe to be the minority view in the Black community. However, a significant segment of the Black community subscribes to this theory. In order to reach this segment of the Black community, we must tear down this cultural and Caucasian Christ and put in the place of Sallman's portrait the biblical and historical Jesus, so that men, women, boys and girls "may see Jesus more clearly, love Him more dearly and follow Him more nearly day by day."

Will the real Jesus stand up? Historically speaking, the real Jesus was not born in Europe, nor was he a product of the Europeans. He was born in the Middle East (Bethlehem) and was embraced by people of African, Semitic and European descent. Jesus was the fulfillment of many Old Testament prophecies regarding the Messiah who was to come (Isaiah 9:6). Jesus identified with common people and they received Him gladly.

Ethnically speaking, Jesus was a mestizo – a person of mixed ancestry. Jesus was primarily Semitic. Semitic people ware usually classified as Caucasians. However, there are five ladies mentioned in the genealogy of Jesus Christ (Tamar, Rahab, Ruth, Bathsheba, and Mary) (Matthew 1:1-16). The first four ladies mentioned are of Hamitic descent. Therefore, Jesus can be claimed ethnically by people of Semitic, Hamitic and Caucasian descent.

Oh, the wisdom of God in sending his son Jesus through the lineage of Shem (Luke 3:23-38). Descendants of Shem are usually dusky or olive-colored. The Bible describes his hair as like lamb's wool (Daniel 7:9). This description of his hair is certainly consistent with the image of Jesus that appeared on the Justinian coin of 750 A.D.

Yes, Jesus the Son of God and Saviour of the world, if he so chose to accept my dinner invitation, would sit down at my table as a man of Semitic and Hamitic descent, hair like wool, dusky or olive-complexioned; and in the Western world, because of his Semitic features and nationality (Israel), would probably be classified as a Caucasian. "For God so loved the world that He gave his only begotten son that whosoever believeth in Him should not perish but have everlasting life" (John 3:16). It is only befitting that the historic Jesus reflect features of all the men in the world because he loves all the people of the world and would have them saved and come to the knowledge of the truth (2 Peter 3:9). He Apostle John was exiled to the isle of Patmos for the Word of God (Revelation 1:9). While at Patmos, John was granted a glimpse of the gloried Saviour (Revelation 1:10-17). In Revelation 1:14, 15, John gives us a description of the glorified Son of God.

> His head and his hair were white like wool, as white as snow, and his eyes were a flame of fire; and his feet like unto fine brass, as if they burned in a furnace; and his voice as the sound of many waters. (Revelation 1:14; 15 KJV)

John used the word "white" twice in these two verses to describe the physical features of Jesus Christ. Permit me to define this word "white" based on the original Greek word "Leukon(s)" translated "white" twice in this verse. In *Vine's Expository Dictionary of Old and New Testament Words*, pages 212 and 213, we discover that "Leukos" is an adjective describing a color that can be compared to "ripened grain." This same word "Leukos" is also found in John 4:35 as a reference to ripened grain. The Greek word "Lampros" is translated "white" in Revelation 15:6 to describe "white linen." A *Greek English Lexicon of the New Testament*, page 472, by Arndt, Giugrich and Bauer, explains that the word "Leukon(s)," Greek for white, included for the Greek many shades of that color and gives as an illustration our "white" wine. John tells us his feet were like unto brass. Brass, ripened grain and white wine are all similar color. This apparently was the color of the glorified Christ, which is consistent with the meaning and complexion of Shem and Semitic people, "dusky" and "olive-colored." Caucasian Christians usually portray Jesus in their paintings as a man with Caucasian features. Hamitic Christians in recent years usually portray Jesus in their paintings as a man with Negroid features. It will do Black and White Christians well who have strong feelings about this issue to hear the words of Tom Skinner:

> One thing is certain; whatever contemporary man decides about the "color" of religion, Christ stands outside the debate. He was God in the form of man – neither Black nor White.

The historical Jesus is the Holy Son of God. He came to reveal God, redeem man and reign over our hearts. Regardless of his complexion and physical features, I'm glad that through Jesus Christ God demonstrated his love for all mankind in that while we were yet sinners, Christ died for us (Romans 5:8), the just for the unjust (1 Peter 3:18) that were might be made the righteousness of God in Him (2 Corinthians 5:21). I'm glad that I've met the Holy and historical Jesus by faith. Have you?

CHAPTER 8

Answering the Critics of Black Christianity

By the term "Black Christianity," I am referring to persons of African descent who have a clear understanding of the person and work of Jesus Christ, have placed their faith and hope for eternal life in Him, and are committed to sharing their faith in Christ with others. Those of us who are in the business of earnestly contending for the faith that was once delivered t the saints (Jude 1:3) sometimes face questions and criticism regarding our faith form an ethnic viewpoint, to which we at times have difficulty responding. The Bible teaches that Christians are to provide rational and respectful answers to every person who questions our faith in Jesus Christ (1 Peter 3:15). The purpose of this chapter and, in one sense, the entire book, is to equip Christians to intelligently respond to questions and criticisms regarding the Christian faith, particularly "Black Christianity." The first criticism that I want to respond to has to do with the ethnic factor in Scripture.

The Bible is a White man's book

The argument goes something like this: The Bible is a White man's book. It was written by the White man, for the White man, and has been used by the White man to mentally and physically enslave Black people. I will be the first to admit that certain passages in Scripture have historically been used unjustifiably by "White Christians" to promote the ideas of slavery, segregation and Black innate inferiority. A careful study of the Scripture will reveal that the Scripture does not teach any of the aforementioned ideas. Is the Bible a White man's book? I will present three responses to this criticism.

(1) The word "Rome" and its derivations are mentioned only twenty times in the Bible and not once in the Old Testament. The word "Greece" and its derivations are mentioned twenty-six times in the Bible and four times in the Old Testament. Now, let us compare the number of times Hamitic countries or cities are found in Scripture.

The Hamitic city of Sidon (Genesis 10:15) and the Sidonians are mentioned more than seventeen times. Ethiopia is mentioned forty times. The Hamitic Canaanites are mentioned one hundred fifty-three times, and the Hamitic Egyptians are mentioned seven hundred twenty-seven times. There are more than on thousand references to Hamitic cities, countries or people in Scripture. Is the Bible a book about White people only? Was the Bible written by White men only?

(2) There are perhaps as many as forty authors recorded in Scripture. By far the vast majority of the Bible's authors were Semitic. Semitic people are classified by the academic community as Caucasians. However, anthropologically speaking, according to Herbert G. May in an article entitled "The People of the Old Testament World," Hamites and Semites belong to the same general physical type (dolichocephalic). Semitic people range from dark to dusky to bright in complexion. Luke is perhaps the only author in the Bible who would be classified as a son of Japheth (European). Luke was Greek, and he wrote his gospel for the Gentiles. One of the meanings of the word Luke is "fair" or "light." The prophet Zephaniah who wrote one of the books of the Old Testament was a descendant of Cush (Ethiopia), which, according to some scholars, denotes

a person who was a descendant of Africa. For certainty, the following authors of Scripture had Hamitic blood flowing through their veins: Joshua, David, Solomon and Zephaniah.

(3) A related criticism sometimes heard in the Black community goes something like this: The King James version of the Bible has been tampered with. It was translated in England in 1611 by prejudiced and chauvinistic White scholars to promote slavery, racism, sexism and classism. Yes, the original Scriptures were written in Hebrew and Greek, and the most popular version used in the Black community is the King James version. The Bible was translated from Greek to Geez, the native Ethiopian language, in the fourth and fifth centuries by Syrian and Ethiopian scholars. To my knowledge, there are no substantive differences between the Scriptures translated by the Ethiopians in their native tongues and the Scriptures translated by the English over one thousand years later in their native tongue. Furthermore, no translation is as accurate as the original.

I believe in the inerrancy of the Scriptures in their original languages. I believe the King James version of Scripture is authoritative. Many people are not aware that the rulers and yardsticks purchased at their local hardware stores are not "accurate." The official measurements and rulers are housed in a government building in Washing, D.C. The yardsticks and rulers that you and I purchase would be minutely slightly different from the official measuring devices housed in Washington. But just as the yardsticks and rulers that we purchase are sufficient and reliable for us to use as an authoritative measuring device, the King James version of the Bible is a reliable, trustworthy document to give us guidance and direction in the Christian life.

Caucasian Christians have historically practiced racism

This is true. A segment of the Caucasian Christian community has practiced racism. Some have acknowledged their racist past and policies and have since recanted and repented. There are others who still sincerely believe even in this day and time that the Black man is biblically cursed.

According to Howard Thurman, the author of the hymn "Amazing Grace" (John Newton) made his money from the sale of slaves to the new world. Thurman further reveals that one of the British slave vessels was named "Jesus." In the Dred Scott Supreme Court Decision, it was decided here in America that a Black man was something less than a man. This same court opened in prayer with a Bible present.

But as far as I am concerned, the hypocrisy and racism practiced by a certain segment of the Caucasian Christian community is no grounds for me to reject Jesus Christ as the Son of God and Savior of the World. It was not a cultural Jesus or a Caucasian Jesus I accepted, but rather a caring Jesus, a comforting Jesus, a compassionate Jesus, a forgiving Jesus, a wonderful Saviour, an everlasting Father, a mighty God and a Prince of Peace (Isaiah 9:6). I would not trade anything for Jesus. As my forefathers said, "I wouldn't take nothing for my journey right now." If I looked at historic institutional Christianity, divorced from biblical and classical Christianity, perhaps I could have been negatively influenced by this line of thinking. I agree with one of my deacons: It's too late for anybody to come to another doctrine or 'gospel.' I know in whom I've believed and am persuaded that He is able to keep that which I have committed unto Him against that day" (2 Timothy 1:12). My faith is not in the institution of Christianity but in an individual named Christ.

My hope is built on nothing less than Jesus blood and his righteousness. I dare not trust the sweetest frame but wholly lean on Jesus' name. ON Christ the solid rock I stand. All other ground is sinking sand.

Islam is the natural religion of the Black man

The final criticism of Black Christianity that I want to address is the teaching that Islam is the natural religion of the Black man and Christianity is the religion of the Europeans. I will not address the latter part of the criticism because I believe I have already sufficiently refuted that position. It is the idea that Islam is the natural religion of the Black man and Christianity was first introduced to the Black man here in America as a means of making the slaves docile that I shall refute in concluding this final chapter. First, a brief overview of the movement.

The modern day architect of the Black Muslim faith here in America was a Black man named Elijah Muhammed. He was born in Sandersville, Georgia, and knew firsthand the injustices and racism to which Blacks were subjected.

He was born Elijah Poole, the son of a Baptist preacher, but was later converted to a Black American version of Islam in the 1930s by the founder of the movement in America (W.D. Farad, sometimes spelled Fard). The forerunner of the Black Muslim movement in America was an uneducated man by the name of Timothy Drew. Somehow, Drew, a native of North Carolina, learned enough about Islam by 1913 to establish a school in Newark, New Jersey, to promote his understanding of Islam. HE viewed Islam as the key to Black liberation here in America. He was born Timothy Drew in 1866, but after his conversion to "Islam" he changed his name to Noble Drew Ali. The contemporary proponent and leader of this movement is Louis Abdul Farrakhan (also spelled Farrakan). Elijah Muhammed, W.D. Fard and Noble Drew Ali converted to Islam and sought and succeeded in getting other Black men and women to convert to Islam on one basic premise: "Islam is the natural religion of the Black nation." In Elijah Muhammed's book, *Message to the*

Black Man in America, we find the gist of his basic teaching:

> Do not tell us that you have "unity and peace" in the white race's religion called Christianity...Many of you sing, "Give me that old time religion." Islam is that "Old time religion."

Unfortunately, Black Muslims in America have persuaded thousands of Blacks to their way of thinking, including prominent Black entertainers, athletes and educators. I respectfully say to anyone who holds the view "Islam is the natural religion of the Black man" that one has to be ignorant of history or the Bible or both to hold this viewpoint. The great Black historian, Dr. W.E.B. Du Bois, articulated my basic response to this criticism in a historically accurate and eloquent manner:

> The Cross preceded the crescent in some of the remotest parts of Africa.

The crescent is a symbol of the Islamic faith comparable to our cross. I shall respond very briefly and to the point of this criticism because this entire book responds to the issue. There are six basic reasons why I hold that Islam is not the "natural religion of the Black nation":

(1) Christ was born in the first century. Muhammed was born in the sixth century.
(2) Consequently, Blacks were committed to Christ first. In Acts 13:1, 2 African men obviously played a significant role in the early Christian movement.
(3) The Judeo-Christian Bible is older than the Qur'an. Islam acknowledges Muhammed borrowing a portion of the Qur'an from the Judeo-Christian Bible. Blacks in Ethiopia were students of the Scripture and had built

69

churches on African soil before Muhammed was ever born.

(4) The spread of Islam was political and economic as much as it was spiritual. When Islam militarily spread over much of Asia and Africa, it became economically and vocationally feasible for all persons in these areas to convert to Islam. The political and economic systems in these countries became inextricably combined with Islam. Consequently, most of Asia and much of Africa converted to Islam as a result of the Arabic conquest. Nevertheless, Dr. Du Bois informs us that Nubians (Ethiopians) who had converted to Christ literally engaged in warfare against the predominantly Arab Muslims to stop the spread of Islam.

(5) Arab Muslims enslaved Blacks. The most shocking and revealing discovery of the one hundred-plus books that I have read or consulted in preparation for this work was learning that Arab Muslims enslaved Blacks and was the first nation to target Blacks exclusively for slavery. The Europeans adopted the practice of targeting Blacks for slavery from the Arab Muslims. I found this extremely shocking because the Black Muslim movement in America was largely built on the premise that Islam and Arabs were ethnically identified, friendly, respectful and hospitable toward Blacks; while Christianity was ethnically identified with Europeans wand a party to the system that sought to control and deny Black people human dignity and freedom. Du Bois informs us that when Black slaves converted to Islam, they won respect in Arab countries. In Islamic law, it was illegal for a true Muslim to hold another Muslim in slavery. Many Blacks converted to Islam in order to receive favorable treatment in Arab Muslim-ruled countries. I wonder if the majority of

Black Muslims in America are aware of the racist history of Arab countries and the real reason why many Blacks "converted" to Islam.

Theologically speaking, it is absurd to suggest that Black Christians reject Christ and Christianity and convert to Islam because of historic racism in institutional Christianity. Even if a person were willing to fall for such simple logic, the Arab Muslim faith, because of its racist history, does not offer an acceptable alternative.

(6) Lamin Sanneh, an assistant professor at Harvard University, in his book *West African Christianity*, documents that Christianity had reached West Africa prior to the West Africans coming to America as slaves.

Based on the aforementioned facts, I conclude that Islam is not the natural religion of the Black nation. It is easy to document contradiction and inconsistencies in institutional Islam and Christianity. Theologically speaking, in Islam man is searching for God, in Christianity God came down to search for man (Luke 19:10). In Islam men are saved by works. In Christianity men are saved by grace. Won't you accept God's grace by faith through Jesus Christ? "Believe on the Lord Jesus, and thou shalt be saved" (Acts 16:31).

CHAPTER 9

In Search of a Name: African American?
Black? Negro? Or Other?

WHAT IS THE PROPER APPELLATION (NAME DESIGNATION) FOR PEOPLE OF AFRICAN DESCENT HERE IN AMERICA? After many years of discussion, this question is still unresolved. I am not under any illusion that I will settle this issue; however, in light of current discussions and as a summary to this book, I decided to address this question. If persons of African descent in America are ever to reach a consensus regarding this issue, it must be addressed with regard to all the historical and technical facts related to the issue. I will trace the names of dark-complexioned people from the beginning of time until this present hour.

In the ancient and classical world, there were eight basic name designations for dark-complexioned persons: Cushites, Hamites, Phutites, Canaanites, Blackheaded ones, Libyans, Ethiopinas and Moors. The words "Cushite" and "Hamite" mean "the Black people." The Phutites, along with the Cushites, Hamites, Canaanites and Sumerians, are listed in the Bible (Genesis 10:6-10) in the Hamitic (Black) family of nations. The Sumerians (Mesopotamians), who were the founders of civilization as we know it today, describe themselves in their own writings as "the blackheaded ones.: These were names dark-complexioned people gave to themselves. Later, the Greeks renamed the land and people of Cush "Ethiopia." The people who called their land "the land of Ham" and themselves "Hamites" were renamed "Egyptians" by the Greeks. The Phutites were renamed "Libyans." And the land and people of Canaan were named by the Greeks "Palestine" and "Palestinians." Eventually, all dark-complexioned people were referred to by the Greeks as Ethiopians- "a man with a (sun) burned face." Generally speaking, in the ancient and classical world dark-complexioned people were known as "the Race of Ham" or "Ethiopians." In the Middle Ages, certain dark-complexioned people throughout Europe, Africa and Asia, who were in many instances of Arab and African descent, were known as "Moors." The word "Moor" means "Black" and was often used as a reference to all dark-complexioned people throughout the globe.

In the modern period, the three most prominent name designations for dark-complexioned people, particularly in America, are African American, Black and Negro. The exact derivation of the name "Africa" is uncertain, but the word was prominently used by the Romans to designate the region around Carthage and later the entire continent. The largest tribe in the region was the Aourigha (pronounced Afarika), and it is probable that this name was the source of the word. The word "Africa" means "dark." It was first used prominently by the Romans, and some say the word is of Roman origin.

Many people argue that the appellation "Black" is baseless. However, the native inhabitant of Ethiopia, Egypt and Sumer (Mesopotamia) named themselves "Black" or "Blackheaded ones."

According to one prominent anthropologist (Arthur Custance, Ph. D., who happens to be White), they came to equate the term "blackheaded people" with the idea of "men" as a real people by contrast with other human beings who are not really men at all.

Perhaps their attitudes were derived from the fact that numerically, politically and culturally they were the dominant people in the ancient world (4000 B.C.-2350 B.C.). {Prejudice is wrong regardless of who is practicing it}. From the beginning of time, the word "Black" has been used by dark-complexioned people and others as an appellation.

According to J.A. Rogers, a distinguished Black scholar, the term "Negro" is a derivative of the word "Niger," and simply means "black." Rogers further maintains that contrary to popular scholarly opinion, the word Niger was not originally a Latin or European term, but an African language. There is a Niger River in Africa and countries called Niger and Nigeria. The term "Niger" is also found in Scripture (Acts 13:1, 2) as a reference to church leaders of African descent who ordained the Apostle Paul to take the gospel to Europe. Adewunni Williams reports that in his native Nigerian tongue, the word "Inago" is somewhat similar in spelling and sound to the word "Negro," and is identical in meaning – "Black man." According to Rogers, there was nothing inherently negative with reference to Black people within the etymology or original usage of the words "Niger" or "Negro." The Europeans borrowed these terms from Africans. The terms "Niger," "Negro," "Black" and "African" are etymologically the same – originating form African languages and meaning "Black" or "Dark." There is absolutely no etymological connection between the African words "Niger" and "Negro" and the English words "niggard" or "nigger." Unfortunately, these words have been misconstrued and mispronounced. The word "Negro" was first used prominently by the Egyptians, and the root word "Niger" and the word "Inago" are Nigerian terms. Thus the words "Negro," "Niger," and "Inago" are distinct African terms.

So what is the proper name designation for persons of African descent here in America? In the final analysis, each person must decide for himself or herself. One must choose the term that is least offensive to his or her sensibilities. There is a context in which I proudly answer to all of these terms (African-American, Black and Negro). Psychologically and emotionally, I am extremely proud of my African descent. Nationally and culturally, I am proud to be an American. The word "Black" etymologically and ethnically connects me with the ancient Cushites (Ethiopians), Sumerians (Blackheads) and Hamites (Egyptians), who were the prominent people of ancient history. My complexion is literally "black," of which I'm also proud. I also proudly answer to the term "Negro." Why? Because I understand the historicity and etymology of the term. The appellation Negro (Niger) encompasses my African roots and biblical roots (Acts 13:1) and etymologically links me with dark-skinned persons throughout the globe who do not necessarily trace their roots back to Africa. Finally, if the word Negro was good enough for Dr. W.E.B. Du Bois, the first Black to graduate with a Ph.D. in history from Harvard University; and the word Negro was good enough for Dr. Martin Luther King, Jr., who used the term often and proudly; and if the word Niger or Negro was good enough for the pages of Scripture (Acts 13:1), then the word Negro is good enough for me. Historically and ethnically, I am proud to be a Negro. However, I repeat: There is a context in which I proudly answer to all of these terms.

Finally, if anybody ask you who I am and you can't remember Cushite or Hamite or Phutite or Ethiopian or African-American or Negro or Black, tell them there is another name that I prefer above all of these. Tell them through faith in the Lord Jesus Christ, I am a child of God; tell them I am a Christian. Tell them I have named the name of Christ and He has named me. In the final analysis, there is only going to be one important name, and that is the name Christ or Christian; this is the name that I must joyfully and proudly answer to and identify with. The name "Christian" connects me with people of every kind, race and tongue. Those of us who share this name will one day spend eternity sharing the joys of heaven.

ABOUT THE AUTHOR

William Dwight McKissic, Sr. is the son of a pastor and a retired school teacher. He is a product of the Pine Bluff, Arkansas public school system, the University of Arkansas at Pine Bluff (formerly A.M. & N. College), and a 1978 graduate of Ouachita Baptist University with a B.A. degree in Religion. He has studied toward the Master of Divinity degree at the Southwestern Baptist Theological Seminary in Fort Worth, Texas.

McKissic accepted Christ at an early age and surrendered to preach at age seventeen. He presently serves as pastor of the Cornerstone Baptist Church of Arlington, Texas, located in the heart of the Dallas/Fort Worth Metroplex. He formerly pastored the St. Peter's Rock Baptist Church of Pine Bluff, Arkansas.

He is married to Vera Nelson McKissic. To this union four children have been born: William Dwight, Jr., James Emory, Carla Danielle and Rosa Michelle.

SELECTED BIBLIOGRAPHY

Adamo, David Tuesday. THE PLACE OF AFRICA AND AFRICANS IN THE OLD TESTAMENT AND ITS ENVIRONMENT. Ann Arbor, Mich.: UMI Dissertation Information Service, 1986.
BLACK WOMEN IN THE BIBLE. 1987.
THE BLACK PROPHET. 1987.
THE BLACK SECRETARY IN THE BIBLE.

Augustine. CITY OF GOD. Edited by Vernon J. Bourke. Garden City, N.J.: Image Books, 1958.

Beck, Melinda, and Dorinda Elliot. NEWSWEEK. New York, N.Y.: Newsweek Inc., Jan. 9, 1989.

Bryant, T.A. TODAY'S DICTIONARY OF THE BIBLE. Minneapolis, Minn. Bethany House Publishers, 1982.

Burns, Edward McNall. WORLD CIVILIZATIONS. New York, N.Y.: W.W. Norton and Company, 1982.

Custance, Arthur C. NOAH'S THREE SONS. Grand Rapids, Mich.: Zondervan Corporation, 1975.

Davies, Clem. THE RACIAL STREAMS OF MANKIND. Los Angeles Calif.: Graphic Press, 1946.

Douglas, J. D. THE INTERNATIONAL DICTIONARY OF THE CHRISTIAN CHURCH Grand Rapids, Mich.: The Zondervan Corporation, 1974.

Draper, James T. FOUNDATIONS OF BIBLICAL FAITH Nashville, Tenn.: Broadman Press, 1979.

Du Bois, W.E.B. THE NEGRO. New York, N.Y.: Oxford University Press, 1970.

Fausett, A. R. FAUSETT'S BIBLE DICTIONARY. Grand Rapids, Mich.: Zondervan Publishing House, 1977.

Finch, Charles, M.D. "Africa and Palestine in Antiquity" article appearing in AFRICAN PRESENCE IN EARLY ASIA. Editors: Ivan Van Sertima and Runoko Rashidi: New Brunswick, N.J.: Transaction Books, 1988.

Garrett, William. NATIONAL GEOGRAPHIC, VOL. 174, No. 4. October 1988, National Geographic Society. Washington, D.C.

Gonzalez, Nancie. SOJOURNERS OF THE CARIBBEAN. Chicago, Ill. University of Illinois Press, 1988.

Hallo, William and William Simpson. THE ANCIENT NEAR EAST. New York, N.Y.: Harcourt Brace Jovanovich, Inc., 1971.

Hansberry, Leo. AFRICA AND AFRICANS AS SEEN BY CLASSICAL WRITERS. Washington D.C.: Howard University Press, 1981.

Hansberry, William L. AFRICA AND AFRICANS, VOL. II. Edited by Joseph E. Harris. Washington D.C.: Howard University Press, 1981.

Hansberry, William L. PILLARS IN ETHIOPIAN HISTORY

VOL. I. Edited by Joseph E. Harris: Washington, D. C.: Howard University Press, 1981.

Harrison, Roland. INTRODUCTION TO THE OLD TESTAMENT. Grand Rapids, Mich.: Erdmans Publishing Company, 1969.

Hicks, H. Beecher. PREACHING THROUGH A STORM. Grand Rapids, Mich.: Zondervan Publishing House, 1987.

Hislop, Alexander. THE TWO BABYLONS. Neptune, N.J.: Loizeaux Brothers, 1959.

Hyman, Mark. BLACKS WHO DIED FOR JESUS. Philadelphia, Pa.: Corrective Black History Books, 1983.

Jackson, John G. ETHIOPIA AND THE ORIGIN OF CIVILIZATION. Baltimore, Md.: Black Classic Press,1978.

Jackson, John G. INTRODUCTION TO AFRICAN CIVILIZATIONS. Secaucus, N.J.: The Citadel Press, 1970.

Johnson, Johnnie L. THE BLACK BIBLICAL HERITAGE. Berkely, Mo.: A & J Enterprise, 1985.

Katz, William L. BLACK INDIANS New York, N.Y.: Ethrac Publications Inc., 1986.

Kiel, C.F. and F. Delitzsch. COMMENTARY ON THE OLD TESTAMENT VOL. I THE PENTATEUCH. Grand Rapids, Mich.: Erdmans Publishing Co., 1983.

Kinder, Derek. GENESIS. Downers Grove, Ill.: Intervarsity Press, 1967.

Lincoln, C. Eric. RACE RELIGION AND THE CONTINUING AMERICAN DILEMMA. New York, N.Y.: Hill and Wong, 1984.

Matson, T. B. THE BIBLE AND RACE. Nashville, Tenn.: Broadman Press, 1959.

Mbiti, John S. AFRICAN RELIGIONS AND PHILOSOPHY. Great Britain: Morrison and Gibb Ltd. London, 1969.

McCall, Emmanuel L. BLACK CHURCH LIFE STYLES. Nashville, Tenn.:Broadman Press, 1986.

McDowell, Josh; John Gilchrist; and Ahmed Deedat. THE ISLAM DEBATE. San Bernardino, Calif.: Here's Life Publishers, 1983. Campus Crusade for Christ.

McGhee, J. Vernon. THROUGH THE BIBLE GENESIS. Nashville, Tenn.: Thomas Nelson, Inc., 1981.

Morris, Henry M., Ph.D. THE GENESIS RECORD. Grand Rapids, Mich.: Baker Book House, 1976.

Muhammad, Elijah. MESSAGE TO THE BLACK MAN. Philadelphia, Pa.: Hakim's Publication, 1965.

Nash, S. C. EBONY ON THE SCENE. Dallas, Tex.: SCN Ministries Publication, 1989.

Phillips, John. EXPLORING GENESIS. Chicago, Ill.: Moody Press, 1980.

Pink, Arthur W. GLEANINGS IN GENESIS. Chicago, Ill.: Moody Press, 1981.

Rhodes, Rev. Dr. F. S. BLACK CHARACTERS AND REFERENCES OF THE HOLY BIBLE. New York, N.Y. Vantage Press, 1980.

Rogers, J.A. 100 AMAZING FACTS ABOUT THE NEGRO WITH COMPLETE PROOF. Helgo M. Rogers, 1970 edition.

Ross, Allen P. CREATION AND BLESSING. Grand Rapids, Mich.: Baker Book House Co., 1988.

Sayce, A. H. THE RACES OF THE OLD TESTAMENT. London, England: Whitefriars Press, 1925.

Scott, Manuel L. THE GOSPEL FOR THE GHETTO. Nashville, Tenn.: Broadman Press, 1973.

Sertima, Ivan (Editor) AFRICAN PRESENCE IN EARLY EUROPE. New Jersey: Rutgers--The State University, New Brunswick, 1985.

Skinner, Tom. HOW BLACK IS. THE GOSPEL? Philadelphia and New York: J. B. Lippincott Co., 1970.

Smith, Sid. WORKING WITH BLACK SOUTHERN BAPTISTS. Nashville, Tenn.: The Sunday School Board, 1987.

Snowden, Jr. Frank M. BLACKS IN ANTIQUITY. Belknap Press of Harvard University Press, Cambridge, Mass.: 1970.

Tenney, Merril C. (General Editor) PICTORIAL BIBLE DICTIONARY. Nashville, Tenn.: The Southwestern Co., 1975.

Thomas, Latta. BIBLICAL FAITH AND THE BLACK AMERICAN Valley Forge, Pa.: Judson Press, 1976.

Thurman, Howard. JESUS AND THE DISINHERITED. Richmond, Ind.: Friends United Press, 1949.

Tierny, John; Linda Wright and Karen Springen. NEWSWEEK. New York, N.Y.: Newsweek Inc., January 11, 1988.

Van, Sertima Ivan (Editor). NILE VALLEY CIVILIZATIONS Brunswick, N.J.: Journal of African Civilizations Ltd. Rutger University Press, 1985.

Vos, Howard, F. GENESIS. Chicago, Ill.: Moody Press, 1982.

Webb, James M. THE BLACK MAN. San Francisco, Calif.: Julian Richardson Association, 1984.

Wells, H.G. THE OUTLINE QE HISTORY. Garden City, N.Y.: Garden City Books. Page 107.

Windsor, Rudolph R. FROM BABYLON TO TIMBUKTU. Smith town, N.Y.:1969.

Windsor, Rudolph R. THE VALLEY OF THE DRY BONES. New York: Vantage Press Inc., 1986.

Woolsey, Raymond H. MEN AND WOMEN OF COLOR IN THE BIBLE. Langley Park, Md.: 1977 Heritage edition of the Holy Bible, King James version.

Zodihates, Spiros. THE HEBREW GREEK KEY STUDY BIBLE. Chattanooga, Tenn.: AMG Publishers, 1984.